S. Hrg. 113–462

RENEWED FOCUS ON EUROPEAN ENERGY SECURITY

HEARING

BEFORE THE

SUBCOMMITTEE ON EUROPEAN AFFAIRS

OF THE

COMMITTEE ON FOREIGN RELATIONS
UNITED STATES SENATE

ONE HUNDRED THIRTEENTH CONGRESS

SECOND SESSION

JULY 8, 2014

Printed for the use of the Committee on Foreign Relations

Available via the World Wide Web: http://www.gpo.gov/fdsys/

U.S. GOVERNMENT PRINTING OFFICE

91–142 PDF   WASHINGTON : 2014

For sale by the Superintendent of Documents, U.S. Government Printing Office
Internet: bookstore.gpo.gov   Phone: toll free (866) 512–1800; DC area (202) 512–1800
Fax: (202) 512–2104   Mail: Stop IDCC, Washington, DC 20402–0001

(II)

CONTENTS

RENEWED FOCUS ON EUROPEAN ENERGY SECURITY

TUESDAY, JULY 8, 2014

U.S. SENATE,
SUBCOMMITTEE ON EUROPEAN AFFAIRS,
COMMITTEE ON FOREIGN RELATIONS,
Washington, DC.

The subcommittee met, pursuant to notice, at 2:33 p.m., in room SD–419, Dirksen Senate Office Building, Hon. Christopher Murphy (chairman of the subcommittee) presiding.

Present: Senators Murphy, Shaheen, and Johnson.

OPENING STATEMENT OF HON. CHRISTOPHER MURPHY, U.S. SENATOR FROM CONNECTICUT

Senator MURPHY. Welcome, everyone, to today's hearing on European energy security. This is not a new topic for this committee, but Russia's annexation of the Crimean Peninsula and military activity in eastern Ukraine has brought a new sense of urgency and focus to this debate.

We are happy to have two great panels here today. I and Senator Johnson will give some very brief opening remarks. We will introduce our panel, let you give a summary of your remarks, ask questions, and then seat our second panel of experts.

Russia's status as a regional power is frankly commensurate only to their ability to blackmail and threaten Europe with Russian gas and oil as the weapon of choice. Europe imports about 30 percent of its gas and 35 percent of its oil from Russia. Political decision-making in Europe is dictated in part by the realities of running a continent on power supplied by one ornery, capricious, and unpredictable neighbor. The question is, How much longer will Europe put up with this reality and what can the United States do in the context of the transatlantic relationship to help Europe break free of Russian energy dependence?

The European Commission's most recent energy security strategy reflects concerns that overdependence on Russia may expose governments and businesses to coercion, threats, and higher prices. The strategy proposes action over the medium to long term to increase Europe's own energy production, increase efficiency, decrease demand, pursue renewable energy alternatives, and diversify its supplier countries and routes.

The strategy is admirable, but in today's hearing we will ask whether there is really political will and the funding to implement it. And we will ask whether some energy strategies in Europe, like reducing carbon emissions, actually increase rather than decrease

(1)

dependence on Russian gas. We will also want to know how non-EU countries lying at the critical faultline between Europe and Russia, like Ukraine and Moldova, fit into Europe's plans for energy independence. We will principally examine what role the United States can play in the energy future of Europe.

This is a complicated issue because complex questions of market dynamics and national sovereignty cloud the role sometimes that the United States can play in Europe's energy future. Yes, it makes sense to examine the role United States natural gas can play in weaning Europe off of Russian gas, but so long as the price in Europe is substantially lower than the price that companies can get in Asia, U.S. natural gas will simply flow with the market.

And even when the United States is willing to lead, there is a question of whether our leadership is wanted. During a recent trip to Bulgaria, Senator Johnson, Senator McCain, and I stood with the Prime Minister as he announced a work stoppage on a gas pipeline opposed by the EU that would increase European dependency on Russian gas. It was a breakthrough, but one that was immediately criticized by some, due to U.S. involvement. It struck me that when it comes to showing leadership on an issue like global energy security America stands to be criticized if we do not lead and criticized if we do.

So I look forward to hearing from our panelists today on all of these questions. With that, let me recognize Senator Johnson for his opening remarks.

OPENING STATEMENT OF HON. RON JOHNSON, U.S. SENATOR FROM WISCONSIN

Senator JOHNSON. Thank you, Mr. Chairman.

I would like to thank the witnesses for, first of all, your thoughtful testimony. I received it ahead of time and had a chance to go through it.

Mr. Chairman, you mentioned a word twice, ''reality,'' or ''realities.'' I come from a business background. I have done a lot of strategic planning in my process, and that is always the first step: You have to recognize the reality of the situation. Once you have done that, you have to set achievable goals, and once you have set those achievable goals, you develop the strategy.

What I am hoping to hear out of the testimony today—and I think we have a pretty good shot at it because it looks like that is what you want to talk about—is let us recognize what the reality of the situation is. If we are going to talk about Russia, we first have to recognize what gives Vladimir Putin power is his oil and gas resources and Europe's, quite honestly, growing dependence on those. So let us spend a lot of time talking about the reality of the situation. Then let us start talking about what are achievable goals and what are the priorities in which we need to address those possible achievable goals.

With that, Mr. Chairman, thank you for holding this hearing and I look forward to the testimony.

Senator MURPHY. No overly excessive introductions here. We are very happy to have two administration witnesses with us. Our first panel is: Amos Hochstein, Deputy Assistant Secretary of State for Energy Diplomacy; and Hoyt Yee, Deputy Assistant Secretary of

State for European and Eurasian Affairs. Both of your written statements will be included in the record in their entirety, so we would ask that you please summarize in about 5 minutes so that we can proceed to questions.

We are going to be joined, I think, by other members of the committee as we move forward. As always, a busy day here. We are thankful for your testimony.

Amos, why do we not start with you, and then we will go to Mr. Hochstein and then to Mr. Yee.

STATEMENT OF AMOS J. HOCHSTEIN, DEPUTY ASSISTANT SECRETARY OF STATE FOR ENERGY DIPLOMACY, U.S. DEPARTMENT OF STATE, WASHINGTON, DC

Mr. HOCHSTEIN. Thank you, Chairman Murphy and Ranking Member Johnson and members of the subcommittee. I appreciate the opportunity to be here today to discuss European energy security during this critical time. The Department of State and the administration as a whole are committed to improving Europe's energy security and we are working closely with our partners in this effort.

Let me begin with an update on the energy crisis in the Ukraine. Ukraine has been negotiating with Russia and the European Union to resolve the issue of price, debt, and future payment for Ukraine's gas imports from Russia. Russia unfortunately ceased supply of gas to Ukraine on June 15, showing little willingness to continue negotiations until Ukraine pays off its debt. The situation is urgent. While Ukrainian production is sufficient to cover summer demand, without Russian gas Ukraine will not be able to meet its consumption needs when the heating season returns.

Although the United States is not party to the trilateral gas negotiations, we are working closely with Ukraine and the EU to identify solutions that will bring an end to the current crisis and make the Ukrainian and EU gas supply system more resilient in the future. EU Energy Commissioner Gunther Oettinger, his cabinet, and DG Energy have done an incredible job and we are in weekly contact with him and his staff, as well as with Minister Prudan of Ukraine, on this issue.

Looking forward, part of the answer for Ukraine's energy security is its integration into the EU energy market. However, before this integration can happen successfully it is essential that Ukraine reform its energy sector. If it does not, if corruption and inefficiency continue along with crippling energy subsidies for consumers, Ukraine will be right back where we all started just a short while ago.

We are working to develop and implement programs to increase Ukraine's energy production and efficiency. Our Bureau, the Energy Resources Bureau at the State Department, is overseeing projects to boost gas production from existing fields, strengthening transparency and management of operations and revenue management at Ukraine's state-owned oil and gas company. We are also working to build the government's capacity to manage the implementation of production-sharing contracts for unconventional gas exploration and development.

To address energy efficiency, USAID's program is designed to enhance Ukraine's energy security as well as reduce and mitigate emissions resulting from the poor use of energy resources in Ukrainian municipalities.

Fortunately, flows of gas through Ukraine to Europe have not been impacted yet. Russia and Ukraine have both promised not to disrupt transit and the short-term impact of this cutoff has been relatively small in Europe. But that is because it is not in the gas-intensive heating season and because we have just gone through a relatively mild winter, so stocks are unseasonably high. But it is critical that countries with storage capacity use these summer months to aggressively increase their supplies. We are working with the Department of Energy as they coordinate an effort to assist the most vulnerable central and southeastern European countries to assess contingency plans in case of a shutoff.

Mr. Chairman, the lack of immediate alarm in Europe cannot lead us or the EU to become passive in addressing a long-term solution. While the media and others have focused on energy security in Europe only for the last several months, as you stated, Mr. Chairman, in your opening statement, this committee, Congress, and the administration have been working on this for quite some time.

As early as the late 1990s, we were heavily engaged in negotiations that made the BTC, the Baku-Tbilisi-Ceyhan pipeline, a reality despite the skepticism of experts who said Azeri oil would never flow to European markets. It probably could not have happened without U.S. leadership.

Our European energy security efforts intensified after Russia cut off gas supplies to Ukraine and European customers in 2009. Since then we have intensely focused on energy security in Europe, advocating energy diversification, particularly in central and Eastern Europe. We work hand in hand with the Commission and with our other allies and energy envoys in Eastern and Central Europe. In fact, DAS Yee and I just returned from Hungary and Croatia last week.

Energy diversification in Europe is critical. This concept includes having broad fuel mix and diversifying the routes as well as the sources of the imports. I am not suggesting that countries should eliminate Russian imports. Russia will and should remain a central player in the region as a producer and as an exporter. But alternative supplies and additional delivery routes will promote competition and increase security.

We are therefore working with our friends and allies, with actions as well as words. Without U.S. engagement the Southern Gas Corridor from Azerbaijan would not be on the verge of becoming a reality.

We agree with our European allies on the critical need for Europe to improve its energy infrastructure by constructing new pipelines, upgrading existing pipelines, upgrading interconnectors to allow bidirectional flow, building new LNG terminals to diversify fuel sources. We applaud the recent announcement of the Hungary-Slovakia Interconnector. Lithuania and Poland are completing their terminals that will come on lie by the end of the year. A proposed terminal on Krk Island in Croatia would bring in supplies from the south. With the completion of reverse flow from Hungary, Croatia could become a gas import hub for southeast Europe and the Balkan States.

Hungary can provide an important link for alternative gas supplies to Ukraine from Croatia. When DAS Hoyt Yee and I were in Croatia and Hungary last week, we encouraged the two countries to work out their differences and to work more closely to address their mutual potential.

We are working closely with our colleagues in the EU to advance this infrastructure buildout and we support the EU's efforts to identify and help fund the most critical projects.

We also commend them for their legal reforms. The passage of the Third Energy Package that made sure that regulatory infrastructure was in place to make sure that destination clauses were not crippling their own energy security were put in place and now is the time to make sure that they are implemented.

As Vice President Biden said in Budapest, the development of a secure, diverse, and interconnected energy market in Europe is the next big step for our European colleagues to initiate in the great project of European economic integration.

Thank you, Mr. Chairman, Ranking Member Johnson. I welcome your questions.

[The prepared statement of Mr. Hochstein follows:]

PREPARED STATEMENT OF AMOS HOCHSTEIN

Thank you, Chairman Murphy, Ranking Member Johnson, and members of the subcommittee; I appreciate the opportunity to be here today to discuss European energy security during this crucial time. The Department of State and broader administration are committed to improving Europe's energy security and working closely with our partners to achieve that.

Let me begin with an update on where the energy crisis in Ukraine stands. Ukraine has been negotiating with Russia and the European Union to resolve the issue of price, debt, and future payment for Ukraine's gas imports from Russia. Russia did not accept the compromise position developed by the EU after weeks of negotiations and unfortunately ceased supply of gas to Ukraine on June 16, showing little willingness to continue negotiations until Ukraine pays off its debt. The situation is urgent for Ukraine. While Ukrainian production is sufficient to cover summer demand, without Russian gas Ukraine will not be able to meet its consumption needs when the heating season resumes. As Ukraine is a key transit route for Russian gas to Europe, it is important to note that European supplies have not been impacted; flows of gas through Ukraine continue. The Russian Government has repeatedly said it would not cut supplies that flow onward through Ukraine to Europe, and Ukraine has also promised not to disrupt transit. The short-term impact of this cutoff has been relatively small in Europe because it is not in the gas-intensive heating season and because last year's winter was mild, leaving stocks unseasonably high.

However, current mild alarm in Europe cannot lead us, or our EU allies, to become passive in addressing a long-term solution. On an annual basis, Russia supplies more than half the gas consumed in Ukraine and more than a quarter of the gas consumed in the EU. Although Ukraine is importing small amounts of gas through reverse flows from Hungary and Poland, Russian imports are required to meet increased demand during the winter heating season.

So where does that leave us today? While the media and others have focused on European energy security only for the last several months, the United States Government has been focused on this issue for several years. As early as the late 1990s, we were heavily engaged in negotiations that made the Baku-Tbilisi-Ceyhan pipeline a reality despite the skepticism of experts who said Azerbaijani oil would never flow to European markets.

Our European energy security efforts intensified after Russia cut off gas supplies to Ukraine and European customers in 2009. Since then, the State Department, spearheaded first by the Special Envoy and now by the Bureau of Energy Resources, has been intensely focused on energy security in Europe, advocating energy diversification across the European Continent, particularly in Central and Eastern Europe. We work hand in hand with the EU Commission as well as with the Energy Envoys in Eastern/Central European countries, and meet often with the Visegrad-4+ ("V4 plus") states (Poland, Slovakia, Czech Republic, and Hungary, plus Bulgaria, Romania, and Croatia). In fact, DAS Yee and I just returned from Hungary and Croatia last week.

When we talk about supply diversification in a European context, there are several components that must be addressed. First is fuel mix—countries should use less by increasing energy efficiency and advancing low carbon energy sources like renewables. A diverse fuel mix could also include nuclear energy and domestic production of gas, including pursuing unconventional supplies if the conditions are right, including subsurface (geologic) potential and above-ground considerations like a strong regulatory regime and environmental safeguards.

Second, it is crucial to diversify import routes: ultimately, Europe must build an interconnected pipeline system that allows gas to flow freely throughout the continent. Finally, European countries must pursue diversification of sources away from a dependence on a single supplier. I am not suggesting that countries should eliminate Russian imports—that is neither necessary nor reasonable and Russia will and should remain a central player in the region—but introduction of alternative supplies will promote competition in the energy market. This will ultimately increase energy security while also benefiting consumers.

We, as a government, are working actively with our friends and allies in Europe to promote diversification with actions as well as words. We are supporting their efforts to ensure the Southern Corridor becomes a reality. We are pleased the project achieved the key milestone of securing a Final Investment Decision (FID) in December 2013. We strongly supported the creation of the Greece-Bulgaria Interconnector, which will allow gas from the Southern Corridor to supply Southeast Europe rather than just enter Central and Western Europe via Italy. For the same reason we are supportive of proposals to build an extension of the Southern Corridor from Albania all the way to Croatia via the Ionian-Adriatic Pipeline, once enough gas becomes available, ultimately supplying neighbors Hungary, Ukraine, and others.

We are working closely with colleagues in the EU's Directorate-General for Energy (DG Energy) to advance east-to-west and west-to-east interconnections of infrastructure in Central and Eastern Europe. These efforts are already producing successful projects such as the recent announcement of the Hungary-Slovakia interconnector. We also support proposals to build liquefied natural gas (LNG) terminals at critical points on European coasts, from Poland to Croatia to the Baltics. In short, Mr. Chairman, we agree with our European allies on the critical need for Europe to improve its energy infrastructure by constructing new pipelines, upgrading interconnectors to allow bidirectional flow, and building new LNG terminals to diversify fuel sources.

We commend the European Union for legal reforms that accelerate market integration and promote diversification of fuel types, sources, and routes. Known as the Third Energy Package, these reforms laid the foundation for a common, regulated, and transparent gas market across the EU. The Third Energy Package separates control of energy supplies from the infrastructure that delivers that energy, so natural gas suppliers, for example, must either divest from ownership of pipeline infrastructure or allow an independent operator to manage the pipeline. It gives any purchaser of gas full control over the product, allowing whoever holds title to the energy the right to sell it onward to any other interested customer, thus eliminating destination clauses. And obligatory third-party access eliminates monopoly control over pipelines, allowing any entity to compete to use gas infrastructure to deliver its product to any consumer who seeks to purchase it.

Part of the answer for Ukraine's energy security is its integration into the EU's energy market. However, before this integration can happen successfully, it is essential that, Ukraine reform its energy sector. If it does not, and if corruption and inefficiency continue along with crippling energy subsidies for consumers, Ukraine will be right back where it started before long.

That's why we are working with Ukraine on internal reform, governance, and efficiency improvements. A major precondition for the financial package from the IMF, and for U.S. and European assistance, is Government of Ukraine action to reform its domestic price and subsidies. The interim government is to be commended for passing and beginning to implement these reforms, but it will be up to the Poroshenko government to see them through. It will be necessary to fight corruption in the energy sector, unleash private investment, and stick to consumer price increases to incentivize energy efficiency improvements, all of which will have a major impact on Ukraine's energy security and economic growth. Ultimately, it is up to the

Ukrainian people and their government to achieve this level of domestic reform, but the administration believes it is our responsibility to provide what tools we can to assist them—and ensure the political space to maneuver—wherever possible.

Getting back to the current state-of-play, the United States, although not party to the trilateral gas negotiations, is working closely with Ukraine and the EU to identify solutions that will bring an end to the current crisis and make the Ukrainian and the EU gas supply systems more resilient in the future. EU Energy Commissioner Günther Oettinger, his Cabinet and DG Energy have done an incredible job, and we are in weekly contact with Commissioner Oettinger and his staff, and with Ukrainian Energy Minister Yuriy Prodan, on this issue.

We have worked closely with the governments and pipeline operators of Ukraine, Hungary, Poland, and Slovakia and with European energy companies to see gas flowing west to east from Europe into Ukraine. Thanks in part to these efforts, gas is now flowing from both Poland and Hungary into Ukraine. In late April in Bratislava, with close involvement of the EU and the State Department, the Governments of Ukraine and Slovakia also signed an MOU on reverse-flow—an agreement which will allow gas to begin to flow from Slovakia into Ukraine as soon as September. Although the volumes will be small initially, they could increase significantly over the next year and help Ukraine benefit from Europe's competitive energy market.

In view of the risks to European gas supplies during a dispute between Russia and Ukraine, the G7 energy ministers also agreed to collaborate in support of contingency planning by vulnerable countries for the upcoming winter season met in Rome on May 5–6, 2014. We are working with the Department of Energy as they coordinate an effort to assist the most vulnerable central and southeast European countries to assess their situation and share best practices.

We are also working to develop and implement programs to increase Ukraine's energy production and efficiency. The Bureau of Energy Resources is overseeing a U.S. Government and donor effort to increase private investment to boost gas production from existing fields, strengthen transparency and management of operations and revenue management at Naftogaz, Ukraine's state-owned oil and gas company, and build the Government of Ukraine's capacity to manage the implementation of production-sharing contracts for unconventional gas exploration and development. Within 1 year, we could introduce improved technologies to increase production in existing gas fields. Additionally, the European Bank for Reconstruction and Development (EBRD) will be a primary partner to pilot a new tender to open existing fields up to private sector investment and increase domestic gas production. On unconventional gas, through the Bureau of Energy Resources' Unconventional Gas Technical Engagement Program (UGTEP), we are working with the Government of Ukraine to assist them in preparing and implementing their responsibilities under contracts with international oil companies to increase unconventional gas production in a commercially and environmentally sustainable manner. The U.S. Government also is sending a petroleum geologist to provide advice about unconventional gas exploration. Finally, it is critical that Ukraine reduce the country's energy intensity. Thankfully, the United States has a long history of support for energy efficiency in Ukraine. Most recently, USAID's Municipal Energy Reform Project (MER Project) is designed to enhance Ukraine's energy security as well as to reduce and mitigate GHG emissions resulting from the poor use of energy resources in Ukrainian municipalities.

These efforts complement the work of our European partners. We have encouraged Europe to take other steps. It is critical that countries with storage capacity use the summer months to aggressively increase their supplies.

All of these actions and issues do not operate in a vacuum. To better understand prices and security concerns in Europe, let me say a few words about the global energy context. First, energy demand is rising rapidly in non-OECD countries, particularly in Asia. So developed energy markets will need to content with this increased competition from emerging markets. Second, we anticipate significant new supplies of natural gas coming onto the market in coming years. This jump in natural gas production is led by the United States and Australia, but could soon include dramatic increases from exciting recent discoveries along the eastern coast of Africa, in such places as Mozambique and Tanzania, from Canada, and in the Eastern Mediterranean. These supplies can and should be included in the medium- and long-term diversification plan for Europe. But to make that happen, Europe must implement the kinds of infrastructure improvements I discussed earlier.

We encourage Europe to build new liquefied natural gas (LNG) terminals to increase its import capacity from these emerging suppliers. LNG import capacity is especially needed on the Baltic and Adriatic coasts to bring non-Russian supplies to the Baltic and Central European markets. Lithuania has built an LNG terminal that will become operational in December 2014. Poland's LNG terminal could start operations in early 2015. Estonia and Finland must agree by this summer on a location for a Baltic regional terminal to remain eligible for partial EU funding of the project. A proposed terminal on Krk Island in Croatia would bring in supplies from the south. With the completion of reverse flow with Hungary, Croatia could become a gas import hub for Southeast Europe and the Balkan States. When DAS Hoyt Yee and I were in Croatia and Hungary last week, we encouraged the two countries to work together more closely to address their mutual energy potential. Hungary can provide an important link for alternative gas supplies to Ukraine from Croatia. We urge these three countries to conclude an MOU that commits to deliver of gas from Croatia to Ukraine via Hungary.

The EU has created a list of Projects of Common Interest (PCI) to prioritize trans-European energy projects that cannot be built with commercial financing alone. Projects will be partially funded from a ÷5.85 billion fund for 2014–2020. We support the EU efforts to identify and help fund the most critical projects. It is essential that the EU and individual countries coordinate and implement these projects without delay. We have been in close discussions with the European Commission and with EU Member States from Finland to Hungary to Greece to sustain this momentum.

Mr. Chairman, the United States is committed to improved energy security in Europe, because it is in our own national security interest to do so. This is an administration-wide effort. The Secretary of State and the White House are also directly involved. At the fifth U.S.-EU Energy Council, Secretary Kerry underscored the need to advance diversification efforts for the EU's security and to work in partnership with the EU on Ukraine. President Obama discussed energy security with Polish President Tusk and other regional leaders on his visit last month. And I traveled with Vice President Biden to Romania and Cyprus in May, where he discussed energy security with the leaders of those countries. Mr. Chairman, I'd like to conclude my remarks by quoting what Vice President Biden said publicly in Budapest: ''the development of a secure, diverse and interconnected energy market in Europe is the next big step for our European colleagues to initiate in a great project of European economic integration.''

Thank you. I welcome your questions.

Senator MURPHY. Mr. Yee.

STATEMENT OF HOYT YEE, DEPUTY ASSISTANT SECRETARY OF STATE FOR EUROPEAN AND EURASIAN AFFAIRS, U.S. DEPARTMENT OF STATE, WASHINGTON, DC

Mr. YEE. Thank you, Chairman Murphy, Ranking Member Johnson, for inviting us to testify before the subcommittee on European energy security and for the personal interest you have taken in this issue.

The Ukraine crisis has demonstrated that security has multiple dimensions. Vulnerabilities can come in many forms—the threat of military intervention, the danger of overdependence on energy from an unreliable and at times hostile neighbor, or the cancer of corruption that weakens institutions and undermines security and sovereignty. Russia's provocative actions in Ukraine have reaffirmed the continued importance of NATO's solemn commitment to collective territorial defense enshrined in article 5 of the NATO Treaty. In response, all NATO members have reaffirmed our collective commitment to preserve the security and territorial integrity of the NATO area.

The United States has led in this effort. We have deployed 750 troops to Estonia, Latvia, Lithuania, Poland, and Romania. We have stepped up our fighter jet deployment to Poland and the Baltic region, and we have maintained a continued naval presence in the Black Sea. As the President announced in Poland last month, we are seeking congressional approval for $1 billion of European Reassurance Initiative to build on our current efforts.

Just as the United States has strengthened its presence in the region, each of the other 27 NATO allies has committed personnel and resources to NATO's reassurance efforts. In the runup to the NATO summit in Wales, we are encouraging all members to sustain this demonstration of alliance solidarity and to reverse the worrying slide in defense budgets.

The United States is working hard with Central and Eastern European countries and the European Union to shore up energy security. We have been working to help Ukraine reform its gas sector, increase energy efficiency, develop domestic sources, including shale gas production, and integrate more fully to European energy markets. We are also working with our European allies to increase Ukraine's access to gas through reverse flows in countries like Slovakia.

At the same time, the Ukraine crisis has given new impetus for countries across Europe to step up efforts to diversify their energy sources and supplies, boost storage, develop networks of interconnectors and reverse flow capacity.

As we work with our European allies to shore up a secure, reliable, and competitive supply of energy, the United States is devoting greater resources to fight corruption in the region. In the wake of the situation in Ukraine and Russia, it is time that we treat corruption as a threat to national security and sovereignty. Corrupt elites and oligarchic interests are reaching across national boundaries to support each other and manipulate decisionmaking in strategic sectors. They hollow out border security and military services, leaving countries vulnerable and exposed to outside interference.

That is why we are empowering our embassies to work with governments, civil society, and the business community across Central and Eastern Europe and the Balkans to develop tailored action plans best suited to local conditions. Multilaterally, we are addressing corruption at the G8, the G20, and the OECD. We are supporting regional law enforcement and anticorruption training centers in Prague and Budapest, and we are encouraging all of our European partners to ratify and implement the U.N.'s Convention Against Corruption.

Our national interest is vested in a Europe in which countries are confident that their borders are respected and secure, their access to energy is reliable and ready, and their government is transparent and accountable to the people. We remain committed to working with this subcommittee and Congress in a bipartisan manner toward achieving these objectives.

Thank you.

[The prepared statement of Mr. Yee follows:]

PREPARED STATEMENT OF HOYT YEE

Thank you for inviting me to testify today before this subcommittee on European energy security. I would particularly like to thank Chairman Murphy and Ranking Member Johnson for the personal interest you have taken in this issue. The visits to key European capitals by members of this committee reaffirm that the United States is as committed as ever to security, sovereignty, and dignity of the people of the region. And your most recent visit to Poland, Romania, Bulgaria, and Ukraine demonstrated that bipartisan engagement on the ground can help focus the attention of our allies on strategic issues, like adequate defense spending and energy diversification.

Just over a week ago in Brussels, the world witnessed two important milestones on the road to a Europe "whole, free, and at peace." Moldova and Georgia signed the Association Agreements/Deep and Comprehensive Free Trade Areas with the European Union. Ukraine signed the remaining economic chapters of its AA. All three countries did this in the face of Russia's persistent attempts to derail the process. The same day, Albania was granted EU candidate status—recognition of the hard work and determination by successive governments to make tough choices including economic and political reform. These achievements demonstrate that European capitals from Kyiv to Chisinau, from Tirana to Tbilisi see greater European integration as the best path to security, prosperity, and a better future for their people.

Yet Russia's occupation and attempted annexation of Crimea, its continued destabilizing actions in Donetsk and Luhansk, and Gazprom's gas delivery cutoff to Ukraine are reminders of the acute security risks that the region faces. Europe's energy security must be seen against the geopolitical backdrop. The Ukraine crisis has demonstrated that security has multiple dimensions. Vulnerabilities can come in many forms: the threat of military intervention; the danger of overdependence on energy from an unreliable and, at times, hostile neighbor; or the cancer of corruption that weakens institutions and undermines security and sovereignty.

My testimony today will examine each of these challenges and how United States policy is moving to bolster our allies in their efforts to tackle them. First, I will address how we are providing allied reassurance to frontline states from the Baltic to the Black Sea at this critical time. Second, I will briefly touch on the current European energy security landscape—particularly in Central and Eastern Europe—as awareness of the region's reliance on Russian gas has increased precipitously. DAS Hochstein has addressed this area in greater detail in his remarks. Finally, I will focus on how corruption is infusing so many elements of political and economic life in the region—including the energy sector—and how the United States is mounting new efforts to help countries in the region root it out.

First, the situation in Ukraine has been a wake-up call for the transatlantic community and NATO. Russia's provocative actions in Ukraine and across the region have reaffirmed the continued importance of our solemn commitments to collective territorial defense enshrined in article 5. In response, all NATO members have reaffirmed our collective commitment to preserve security and territorial integrity in the NATO space.

The United States has led in this effort, deploying a persistent, rotational military presence on land, sea, and air in Central and Eastern Europe. We have deployed approximately 600 troops to Estonia, Latvia, Lithuania, and Poland; stepped up our fighter jet deployment to Poland and the Baltic region; and increased our naval presence in the Black Sea. And as the President announced in Poland last month, we are ready to do more. The administration requested congressional approval for a $1 billion European Reassurance Initiative to build on our current efforts. This initiative will allow us to increase exercises, training, and our rotational presence on the territory of our Central and Eastern European allies; enhance prepositioned equipment and improve infrastructure; and elevate our participation in NATO naval force deployments in the Baltic and Black seas. We also intend to build up the capacity of friends like Georgia, Moldova, and Ukraine so that they can work effectively alongside the NATO allies and the United States as well as provide for their own defense.

Just as the United States strengthens its presence in the region, each of the other 27 NATO allies has committed personnel and resources to NATO's reassurance effort. In May, Poland, with augmentation from France, the U.K., and Denmark, took over responsibility for the Baltic Air Policing (BAP) mission from the United States. The BAP mission has tripled the number of planes patrolling the Baltic States and NATO is now flying the mission from two additional locations. In addition, NATO has been flying two of its own AWACS surveillance planes over alliance territory since the beginning of the crisis. At sea, one of NATO's Standing Naval Forces, with ships from Germany, Poland, Lithuania, Estonia, and Denmark are patrolling the Baltic Sea.

In the runup to the NATO summit in Wales, we are encouraging all members to sustain this demonstration of alliance solidarity and reverse the worrying slide in defense budgets. All NATO members must set themselves on the path to meet the 2 percent national defense-spending goal that we, as an alliance, collectively established. Eleven allies have committed to meet this target and four have already done so. We urge other NATO members to join in this effort. As President Obama stated in Warsaw in June, "Just as the United States is increasing our commitment, so must others. Every NATO member is protected by our alliance, and every NATO member must carry its share in our alliance."

Second, the United States is working hard with Central and Eastern European countries and the EU to shore up energy security by increasing energy efficiency, improving regulation, promoting nuclear safety and strengthening regional coordination. The U.S.- EU Energy Council meeting in April, chaired by Secretary Kerry, High Representative Ashton and Commissioner Oettinger, reiterated our joint commitment to these objectives.

Since the onset of the Ukraine/Russia crisis, the U.S. has provided Ukraine with a congressionally authorized $1 billion loan guarantee as well as $133 million in assistance to address the country's most urgent needs. The loan guarantee was targeted at financial support to soften the impact of Ukraine's painful but necessary economic reforms—including gas price liberalization and increased energy efficiency—on the country's most vulnerable. Reducing Ukraine's energy dependence on Russia is one of five top priority areas for U.S. assistance to Ukraine. The United States is working to help Ukraine reform its gas sector, increase energy efficiency, develop domestic sources including shale gas production, and integrate more fully into European energy markets. We are also working with our European allies to increase Ukraine's access to gas through reverse flows from countries like Slovakia.

At the same time, the Ukraine crisis has given new impetus for countries across Europe to step up efforts to diversify their energy sources and supplies, boost storage, develop robust networks of interconnectors and reverse flow capacity. The EU is intensifying its work to create an integrated energy market that increases energy security and competition and lowers prices for its citizens. Countries are committed to building a nuclear power industry, like Poland, or developing greater nuclear capacity, like Bulgaria and Romania. Poland, the Baltic countries and Croatia have Liquefied Natural Gas (LNG) import terminals in development. DAS Hochstein just visited Croatia and Hungary to advance our interests in these areas; he has spoken to our efforts in Ukraine and Europe in greater detail.

Third, as we work with our European allies to shore up a secure, reliable, and competitive supply of energy, the United States is devoting greater resources to fight corruption in the region. As Vice President Biden said in Romania, corruption eats away at society, prosperity, and security of many young democracies across Europe and Eurasia. Across the region, corrupt officials abuse their power to line their pockets, rig procurement contracts, give political favors for cronies, apply justice selectively, and siphon off their countries' economic potential to secret off-shore bank accounts and pet projects. The energy sector is one of the most highly vulnerable to the corrosive effects of this corruption.

From Bosnia and Herzegovina to Romania to the Caucasus, many ordinary people feel cheated by a crooked elite and are expressing their frustration from the ballot box to the public square. In the Czech Republic, a new political party focused on anticorruption surprised observers by coming in second in parliamentary elections, and is now part of the governing coalition. In 2013, corruption drove tens of thousands of Bulgarians to the streets to demand transparency and accountability; similar grievances led to wide protests in major Bosnian cities in February. In Slovenia, corruption contributed to the downfall of the government. And anger at Yanukovych regime's corruption helped drive a million Ukrainians of all stripes into the streets in the dead of winter.

In the wake of the situation in Ukraine and Russia, it is time that we treat corruption as more than a threat to economic prosperity or democratic legitimacy. Corruption doesn't just rot countries from the inside; it is also a threat to national security and sovereignty. Corruption-riddled political systems can play right into the hands of destructive outside influences. Corrupt elites and oligarchic interests are reaching across national boundaries to support each other and manipulate decision-making in strategic sectors. They hollow out border security and military services, leaving countries vulnerable and exposed to outside interference.

That is why we are empowering our embassies to work with governments, civil society, and the business community across Central and Eastern Europe and the Balkans to develop tailored action plans best suited to local conditions. We are convening stakeholders, raising public awareness, building networks, and providing training. We are providing legal advice, technical assistance, and peer-review mechanisms that enable like-minded governments to share anticorruption solutions with each other, support for greater use of e-governance tools, and backing for civil society organizations that place the fight of corruption at the heart of their work. Through coalition building and technology, we can more effectively expose corruption where it festers and make better use of data in pursuing accountability for corruption. And our embassies will work to empower multistakeholder processes to improve transparency and accountability, supporting initiatives like the Open Government Partnership and the Extractive Industries Transparency Initiative.

Multilaterally, we have worked to address these issues in the G8, the G20, and the OECD. We are using reviews by the OECD Working Group on Bribery, its Anti-Corruption Network for Eastern Europe and Central Asia, and the Council of Europe's Group of States Against Corruption (GRECO) to raise awareness of egregious practices; supporting regional law enforcement and anticorruption training centers in Prague and Budapest; and encouraging all of our European partners to ratify and implement the U.N.'s Convention against Corruption.

The United States and the EU are intensifying our joint efforts to tackle this challenge across the region. Both sides of the Atlantic have passed legislation to compel companies to publicly disclose the payments they make to governments in extractive industries such as oil, gas, and minerals—sectors that are particularly vulnerable to corruption. Our aid and technical assistance complements the European Union's work with Ukraine, Moldova, and Georgia as well as the Balkans, which help to chart a path toward stronger rule of law and greater public accountability, key elements in the fight against corruption.

We are also looking at how to use the Transatlantic Trade and Investment Partnership (TTIP) and other trade agreements to confront this challenge. TTIP aims to set a new global gold standard for free trade. In the past, the United States has included specific commitments on anticorruption in other bilateral trade agreements. We should explore fully what might be possible in the context of a comprehensive and ambitious TTIP agreement.

Europe is our largest trading partner and home to some of our longest standing and most important allies. Our national interest is vested in a Europe in which countries are confident that their borders are respected and secure; their access to energy is reliable and ready; and their government is transparent and accountable to the people. We remain committed to working with this subcommittee and Congress in a bipartisan manner toward achieving these objectives.

Senator MURPHY. Thank you to both of you for your testimony.

Mr. Hochstein, you talked about the things that Ukraine needs to do in order to reform its energy markets. This is the most energy-inefficient country in the entire region. I will direct the question to you, but happy to have Mr. Yee respond as well. The reforms they need to undertake are dramatic and the effect of those reforms done too precipitously is perhaps destabilizing in a country right now that does not need much more instability. The vector between what gas prices are today and what they would be without the subsidy is enormous. The amount of money they have to spend on reengineering this wildly inefficient Soviet energy architecture is essentially almost a rip-down and build-back-up proposition.

So how do we ask Ukraine to do this without requiring them to spend money they do not have and impose price increases on citizens who are right now looking for reasons to be confident rather than angry at their new government?

Mr. HOCHSTEIN. Mr. Chairman, those are great questions, and it is a very difficult task to do, but it must be done, because if we do not, as I said in my testimony, if we do not reform it, if we just pour money into this and make sure that there are some reverse flows and gas comes in, as I said before, we are going to be back at this problem again very shortly.

This is an opportunity. It is a moment in time for Ukraine to walk away from its past. Part of its past was a highly corrupt, inefficient system that kept using—instead of using energy as a resource for stability and security, it was the opposite. So we can take this moment in time and, as you said, not dramatically tear it all down and build it back up in a moment during a crisis, but put in place some fences around the energy sector so that it is free of corruption—that you could always do—to start talking about the subsidy reform not as an overnight bring it to market-based

13

pricing, but to see how we can do this efficiently and effectively to begin that process.

How do you look at the entire apparatus of their energy sector so that it reflects good management? If we can do that and make it open and transparent and effective and efficient, we will do a number of things. One, we will be able to actually reduce their costs over time because efficiency rates will go up. Second, they will not get further into the hole by having the subsidies drag them down. Third, they will encourage new investment of international oil companies and other parts of the energy sector worldwide to actually be interested in investing in the sector. Fourth, they will be able to see growth in their production levels. Their natural gas production levels today can be much higher if they use new technologies and a modern way of doing it—and work on the unconventional side. If we could put together a regulatory framework that understands how to do the shale gas exploration in a safe, secure manner, we could bring in the foreign direct investment into that, grow it, and at the end of the day have additional gas sources of their own to contribute to the new reverse flows and new energy diversification that we are going to do elsewhere, in addition to bringing other forms of energy so that the system is more resilient.

So for that, I agree that it is hard to do it all at once. You have to be careful about it. I think that is what we are trying to do.

Senator MURPHY. Mr. Yee, talk to me about how Europe thinks and talks about this issue? We are encouraged by developments like the Third Energy Package, which recognizes the immense problem of allowing Gazprom to both control the source of the energy and the transmission of it. But for every step forward there are steps backward: members of the EU, like Bulgaria, that are openly opposing the Third Energy Package in the way that they are conducting their business; a country like Germany, who just this week announced that they are moving forward or passed— I cannot remember—new legislation that will effectively end for the foreseeable future any potential of developing their own shale gas.

There often seems to be a lack of urgency in Europe about this question, a lot of talk in Brussels, but then not always corresponding action at the individual member state level.

Mr. YEE. Thank you for that question, Mr. Chairman. I would agree that there are different voices that we are hearing in Europe about the specific remedies and measures that need to be taken to address the problems of energy security and also Ukraine's particular case of energy security.

One thing, though, that I think all the members of the European Union, all the countries that I deal with in Europe, share is a desire for energy diversification, a desire for less dependence on single sources, less dependence on Russia. So while they might disagree on the means and some of the measures and the timeframes, there is a general consensus on the need to do something to increase energy security through diversification.

So one thing that we do here is an interest in developing alternative pipelines, alternative routes. We may not always agree on which are the best ones, but we do have a discussion with the Europeans, we have an open dialogue with the Europeans, on the need to develop these alternative routes, in addition to alternative sources.

So the countries which are the most directly dependent on Russia, most dependent on Russian gas, for example, might be slightly less eager to talk about discontinuing South Stream or routes that we feel may not be commercially as viable or long-term best solutions for Europe. But we are having success in discussing with the Europeans the need to diversify, the need to devise alternative routes and sources.

Senator MURPHY. Let me ask you specifically about the Germans, then. The Germans have openly been the most skeptical about sanctions on Russia with respect to action in the Ukraine. They are in the process of dismantling their nuclear fleet, which is a big part of energy independence and diversification. They are making a new commitment against developing their own internal energy resources under their ground, the potential for rather large shale deposits that they are going to leave in place.

It is very hard for the EU to move without an active Germany on these questions. What is your feeling about specifically the German Government's commitment to leading when it comes to some of these questions of EU energy security?

Mr. YEE. Thank you for that question. Our sense is that certainly Germany understands its responsibility as a leading economy and a leader in Europe and the European Union and the need for them to show leadership on the issue of energy security. I think their role reflects in part and the difficulty in reaching a consensus reflects the different situations of the European Union members, each of which has its own set of challenges.

We are seeing from Germany an interest in discussing with us, discussing with the Commission, on ways to find solutions to these problems, certainly in its approach to Russia. Recently, Chancellor Merkel in her meetings with Foreign Minister Lavrov and with the French Foreign Minister has made clear expectation that there has to be some progress in Ukraine, in Russia's approach to Ukraine, to the situation in Ukraine.

We also have discussions with the European Commission, together with the Germans and other European members, on how we can factor in all the different challenges, all the difficulties that European Union members face, whether it is limited—whether it is an overdependence on gas or geographical limitations on what can be done in terms of alternative routes.

Senator MURPHY. Senator Johnson.

Senator JOHNSON. Secretary Yee, in your testimony you mentioned corruption. When Senator Murphy and I went through Poland, the Ukraine, and then to Romania and Bulgaria, that certainly was echoed as a reality of the situation. A legacy of really the Soviet era is just corruption throughout those Eastern European nations. When we visited Poland, I think our sense of the countries we visited was they have probably made the most progress in terms of limiting corruption, and I think they are probably doing better economically as a result of that.

I want to talk a little bit about Romania because I think we were both impressed with the Chargé there, Charlie Butcher. He arranged a meeting initially with us. Our first meeting in Romania was with the Chief Prosecutor General for Corruption, Laura Kovesi, an incredibly impressive, incredibly courageous young woman who is really battling corruption in Romania.

I think we were both concerned that we do not have an ambassador for Romania. The Chargé's term was basically coming up. Is the administration at all addressing that situation? Because I think the only way Romania proceeds in terms of reducing corruption is to have a strong U.S. presence to continue to put pressure on the Romanian Government to certainly protect Ms. Kovesi, who is under death threat.

But can you just speak at all of the administration's plan in terms of American representation to Romania?

Mr. YEE. Thank you, Mr. Ranking Member. Yes, the administration is working to identify an ambassador for Romania, working as quickly as possible to identify the right candidate. We also agree with you, Senator Johnson, that Duane Butcher, our Chargé d'Affaires there, is doing an excellent job. We do agree that there needs to be an ambassador and we are working to get that in place as soon as possible.

Regarding the prosecutor you mentioned, Ms. Kovesi, and the overall effort to fight corruption in Romania, American leadership has been critical. I think our good relations, working relations with the government, even when we disagree with the government of Mr. Ponta, is such that we are able to express our concerns, our objections, when there are steps taken by officials, business people, that are clearly in violation of Romanian law in addition to international rules and principles.

So we have that frank dialogue. We are able to do that with a very strong Embassy team there. I think we need to continue to do that. It certainly helps when Members of Congress also visit these capitals to reinforce the message that we take the corruption very seriously, not only as a matter of economics or of moral principle, but as a matter of national security.

Senator JOHNSON. Until an ambassador is appointed, has the administration considered reappointing or asking Mr. Butcher to stay on?

Mr. YEE. Mr. Butcher will complete his tenure this summer. There is another Chargé d'Affaires who has already arrived at post and is overlapping now with Mr. Butcher and will take over by the end of the summer.

Senator JOHNSON. I am sure Senator Murphy agrees with me, we do not want to see a void there in Romania. It is important that we do not do that.

Mr. Hochstein, you were talking a little bit about developing shale gas in Europe. Does the United States have any estimates or does Europe have any estimates in terms of what their oil and gas potential really is if they were willing to exploit it?

Mr. HOCHSTEIN. Yes, Senator. We work with countries that are interested and, as Chairman Murphy talked about when he used the example of Germany, it is country by country. Every member state in the EU has a very different perspective on different resources, including shale. We had worked very closely with Poland, with Ukraine, with Romania, and we are working with other countries that are interested in pursuing that. We help identify what

16

the shale resource is, using their own resources and the U.S. Geological Survey to be able to conduct a survey to identify what the levels and what the commerciality is of those resources.

Senator JOHNSON. Can you share with me or with the committee what those resources are? What are the estimates? Can Europe be more independent if it were only to, for example, do fracking, actually exploit their shale gas reserves?

Mr. HOCHSTEIN. Again, there is always a difference between what the estimates are and what it becomes in reality. If you look at Poland as an example, there were a lot of published estimates that were quite high. Several companies, international oil companies, including large American companies, went in. The results were more disappointing. Some have already left as a result. Some have remained. So we have to see as the drilling begins and we will see what is happening.

In Ukraine, we are working with them on putting some of those frameworks in place to allow further exploration. They are interested. There are already companies in place. Romania is the same, where you visited. I was there just before the Senate delegation was there with Vice President Biden, talking to them about pursuing their unconventional resources as well as their offshore resources.

So in short, I do not have the figures in front of me. It is something that I can definitely send to your office for you to see what our estimates are. In some places we do not deliver those publicly. But we are working with any country that is interested in doing it, and we have a program at the State Department, the Unconventional Gas Technical Expertise Program, that specifically puts together that framework for countries interested.

Senator JOHNSON. To the best of your knowledge, the companies that went in but have subsequently left, did they leave because the oil and gas reserves were not there, too expensive to develop, or did they leave because of corruption, or some combination of the two?

Mr. HOCHSTEIN. In that case it was not the issue of corruption. It was more about the resource.

Senator JOHNSON. Can you speak to me a little bit about spot pricing versus oil index pricing and the effect that has on the situation in Europe in terms of gas?

Mr. HOCHSTEIN. Europe buys its gas by pipeline from some of their suppliers, and they can buy LNG; they can bring it in as liquefied natural gas through other ports. They have long-term contracts and then there are spot prices. The long-term contracts they have with Russia, for instance, have been renegotiated a couple years ago. Some of them are coming up for renewal.

The price in Europe has traditionally been relatively high. It has come down over the last couple of years. Part of that is because of the shale gas revolution in the United States, other market dynamics around the world. Prices have settled now on somewhere in the $10 to $12. But it is also because there has been fuel-switching in Europe as well. There has been a lot of switchover from gas to coal. And with a mild winter in a region that uses gas primarily for heating, that reduces the need for gas as well.

So a variety of factors come into the pricing. I would not want to suggest that there is one specific cause for pricing. But clearly, if they can improve their infrastructure interconnections—so it is not just about the infrastructure to bring the gas into the continent, but rather for it to flow across from country to country. If you can upgrade the infrastructure in Romania so there could be a flow cross-border, if you could bring interconnnections from Croatia into Hungary, from Slovakia into Hungary, if all those interconnections can happen you can have an integrated market where gas can flow. That will help with price and it will help with stability and security.

Senator JOHNSON. I know I am out of time, but just let me follow up on this. Would moving toward spot pricing be a net positive or a net negative for Europe?

Mr. HOCHSTEIN. That is probably a good question to ask some of my colleagues and friends who are going to testify on the second panel. I would not want to speculate on that. I think that I have learned in this job that speculating on price on oil and gas——

Senator JOHNSON. Are you seeing a trend one way or the other in Europe, a movement toward spot away from oil-indexed?

Mr. HOCHSTEIN. I think it depends on when you ask the question. If you asked me that last year, I probably would have had a different answer about what the trajectory is versus now. I think that the events and how we see events happening in the next few months shaping up—you probably will see a change. But again, I would reserve that for those who are going to speculate.

Senator JOHNSON. Thank you, Mr. Chairman.

Senator MURPHY. Senator Shaheen.

Senator SHAHEEN. Thank you.

Thank you both for being here. The EU has coordinated a number of policies to address particular issues that have come up for the EU as a whole. But it is my understanding that energy decisions are still made on a state-by-state basis; is that correct? And can you talk about how these bilateral energy agreements have complicated the ability to get a collective energy strategy for the region?

Mr. HOCHSTEIN. Senator, you are right, there is a Commissioner for Energy, Commissioner Oettinger. But many parts, many aspects of energy policy, are still set at the member-state level.

The second issue that you raise is the bilateral agreements. It is true that people talk often about Europe's dependency on Russian gas. It is a two-way street. There is a Russian dependency on Europe as a gas market. It is a $50 billion a year gas market, and they have very little infrastructure to support exports outside of Europe.

With those facts, one would normally think that this would equalize the leverage and that there would be a negotiation position based on the consumers in Europe, on that purchasing power. But because there has been a bilateral agreement for each country, that has weakened that position. That is because countries are reluctant to allow a single central EU to negotiate price.

That issue has come up in a proposal by the Prime Minister of Poland, who has suggested to have some kind of energy union, where they can negotiate collectively with Russia. That is a very controversial issue in Europe. There are a lot of different views on that.

I would just note that if you did make decisions centrally in Europe it would have impacts beyond the negotiations of agreements. It would also impact some of the things that Chairman Murphy talked about a moment ago, and that is what do you do about nuclear, what do you do about shale gas? There are very different views. If a decision was made centrally in Europe on fuel sources and what should be allowed, approved, and what should be banned, that could lead in a different direction as well.

So there are pluses and minuses to that idea. But on the negotiation side of agreement, there is no doubt that there would be a benefit.

Senator SHAHEEN. Given the recent events in Ukraine and Russia's response, does that not provide some added impetus to try and encourage more unified action in the EU?

Mr. HOCHSTEIN. I think that, you know, you look at what is happening in Ukraine and its impacts on Europe and the impacts themselves are very different in different countries. If you are receiving your gas through Ukraine, you are going to have one perspective, very different than those who receive their gas from Russia through other means, through other pipelines, and the level of dependency will change your attitude.

It certainly caught our attention after the 2009 crisis, when on January 1 Ukraine's gas supplies from Russia were cut off and then on January 9 the rest of Europe, or the rest of Europe through Ukraine, was cut off. We have been trying to get and working with our EU colleagues to act as though there is still a sense of urgency to be able to diversify.

The Third Energy Package that has been mentioned was a result of that 2009 crisis. We think that it would be a mistake not to take advantage and to seize the day and seize the moment of this crisis to move forward on implementation of a number of issues, specifically on the infrastructure side, but also on coming together as a region and cooperating better.

Senator SHAHEEN. Well, that is the way we see it, but I guess what I am asking is, Do we think the Europeans see it that way and what has been their response?

Mr. HOCHSTEIN. I think it is hard to say the Europeans in this case, because again there are different regions. I think there is by and large, as DAS Yee said, there is a European conventional wisdom that we need to—they need to work on energy security through diversification. What exactly diversification means changes, though. This goes back to, Senator Johnson, when you talked about reality-based. Some countries view diversification in a different way, not just diversifying their sources away from Russia, but also diversifying their routes of getting their gas from Russia. Hence the discussion on South Stream. Some countries see, if I can get my gas from Russia through a different mechanism that is not dependent on the relationship of Russia and Ukraine, maybe that is my solution. It ultimately does not solve the problem, but there is a difference of view there.

Senator SHAHEEN. Well, one area where we know everybody could benefit is through energy efficiency. It is my understanding the EU will be meeting in October to unveil new energy efficiency goals and a framework to attain them. I wonder if you could talk about what we think will be coming out of these talks and whether the member states will be able to accomplish the goals from those talks?

Mr. HOCHSTEIN. Thank you, Senator. Yes, they are going to be— I do not want to presuppose what they are going to say and announce there. They did have an aggressive efficiency rate target for 2020, 20 percent by 2020, which the projections are that they are not going to quite hit, but come pretty close. I think they would like to look at extending that and look at specific measures that would address efficiency. As you said, it is the easiest way to save a dollar, is through efficiency.

Ukraine has one of the worst records in the world on efficiency and we are very much focused on that. But the EU needs to focus more internally. They have already done quite a bit, even though they may miss the target. But we are working with them to understand better how they think they can achieve that and to see if we can be supportive in that.

Senator SHAHEEN. Can you talk a little bit about what the obstacles are? Because I think we are in agreement that efficiency is the first fuel, right, something that is the cheapest, fastest way to deal with our energy needs? So why is this not something that they would embrace, that all member states would embrace?

Mr. HOCHSTEIN. I think in the idea level they all do embrace. It is in the implementation of putting the rules and regulations in place that will allow for it to happen in an effective manner and enforcing the rules and regulations that are there that seems to be more of the challenge. I think part of this is looking, how can you bring all of this into compliance, put in place a regulatory framework and rules that will actually deliver the results that they want.

It is spotty and in some countries they have achieved more than others, and therefore when you look at the EU-wide position it is important to get those rules in place so that everybody can implement it efficiently.

Senator SHAHEEN. So what could we do to help with that on the efficiency front?

Mr. HOCHSTEIN. We have a number of programs that we work with individual countries—again, we do not do it through the EU as a central mechanism, but through individual countries—to look where we can. We have committees with the EU, through the U.S.-EU Energy Council, to look specifically at efficiency standards. There are some great lessons learned here from the United States that we are able to export. They have some ideas of their own and looking at how we can cooperate, bringing our experience to benefit what they are trying to achieve. But there is a lot of work being done and I am happy to send some things over to your office, a list of the programs that we are working on.

Senator SHAHEEN. I would appreciate that. I am sure if Congress would pass energy efficiency legislation that would serve as a good model to share with them; would you not agree?

Mr. HOCHSTEIN. I will follow what Congress does with great interest.

Senator SHAHEEN. Thank you. Very well said.

Senator MURPHY. I just have one additional question for the panel and let me direct it to you, Mr. Hochstein. Senator Markey is not here to give us his sermon on what the export of natural gas will do to prices here in the United States. But let me ask you about what the market barriers are to U.S. natural gas reaching Europe?

The administration is quick to remind us that they are approving licenses here as quickly as they can and others are quick to remind us that there is only 25 percent of capacity being used currently at European terminals and there is another 35-plus terminals that are scheduled to be built.

So with respect to the market, what is the barrier that would stop potentially licensed U.S. natural gas exports from ending up in Europe?

Mr. HOCHSTEIN. Senator, to be honest, I think that you answered your question very well in your own question. At the end of the day, we have provided licenses, granted licenses for over 90 BCM of gas already. These are companies that actually have to now build the infrastructure here in the United States so that they can export it.

Price plays a big role in this, and if you look at what the Henry hub price is today, where European prices are, add what you need to add for transportation, regasification, liquefaction, to Henry hub, to the price, and that will often dictate where this gas will end up for profitability purposes or reasons.

I do not believe that it matters, though, where the individual molecule from the United States will end up. Even if the gas goes to Asia markets, the idea is that American gas will come onto the international market, which will adjust itself and free up gas that was destined for the markets where American gas came and will make those supplies available now to Europe. So even if it is not a contract that is directly signed between an LNG facility in Klaipeda, Lithuania, or elsewhere in Europe, it does not mean that there is no impact of U.S. shale gas exports, gas exports, on the European market.

We have already seen that effect simply by no longer importing the great volumes that we used to or the great volumes that we were projected to import, and those already, by being freed up from the U.S. market to Europe and to Asia, had an impact on price in Europe and even led to the ability of countries and companies in Europe to renegotiate contracts in the last 2 years with Gazprom for the first time.

So I think it is not really a matter of whether there is a direct contract between those, between two end points, but rather how does this affect the market as a whole. I will say that, as I say to my European friends and colleagues when I travel there and they complain about natural gas exports, that the best way to do that is to have companies in Europe negotiate contracts with American companies or operators or distributors here in the United States for already gas that is contracted for India, for Japan, and for others, and that is probably a better way to do it than to think about just the governmental control of it.

Senator MURPHY. I do think, and I hope that you will point out, the curious position that Europe continues to be in, which is to ask vociferously and aggressively for U.S. shale gas and then be totally unwilling to develop their own resources. They seem very happy to receive the resource from the United States, while very unhappy to develop their own resources.

I get it that they have the ability to make sovereign decisions about what domestic resources they will and will not exploit. It is not necessarily a hypocritical position, but it is curious, to say the least.

Mr. HOCHSTEIN. Mr. Chairman, I rarely miss the opportunity to raise that irony in my discussions.

Senator MURPHY. Senator Johnson, any further questions for this panel?

Senator JOHNSON. It might be hypocritical.

I just want to go to nuclear. My understanding is France generates about 75 percent of its power needs through nuclear power. Is that largely correct?

Mr. HOCHSTEIN. Yes.

Senator JOHNSON. What is the activity throughout the rest of Europe in terms of developing nuclear as a clean European alternative?

Mr. HOCHSTEIN. Again, it changes from country to country. There are a number of countries that are working on nuclear energy. Hungary is looking to expand its current nuclear. The Czech Republic has been in a very lengthy process to identify—through the tender process—to identify a company to build and expand nuclear power. That has hit some stumbling blocks in the Czech Republic. Bulgaria is working on it as well.

So there are countries that are working on expanding and promoting nuclear energy. There are others, as Chairman Murphy mentioned, like Germany, that have decided in the wake of the Fukushima disaster to go the other direction.

When we are asked for our opinion in Europe, we clearly say that this is something for each state and each country to make their own decisions. We believe that nuclear energy should be part of the mix, but that is something for a sovereign state to make their own decision. If they so choose to go in the nuclear direction and make that part of their mix, we will be there fully supportive and work with—we believe that we have companies here in the United States that are the best in the world and we believe that it is probably going to be a good decision for energy security for each country to have as many clean energy options as possible.

Senator JOHNSON. What does Europe do with its nuclear waste?

Mr. HOCHSTEIN. I do not have that information in front of me, but again I am happy to get that to you.

Senator JOHNSON. You were mentioning the impact on price, just of the United States importing less oil and gas. Can you put some figures to that trend?

Mr. HOCHSTEIN. We today are not yet a net—we are not a net exporter yet of natural gas. We will be, I believe it is by 2016, we will be a net exporter of natural gas. We today still import some gas. On the oil side, we are far from being independent, as people like to say. We still import significant amounts of oil. However, we have reduced our imports quite significantly, down to the 30-percent range, and a lot of our gas we get still from our hemisphere and from our region, with some quantities coming from Saudi and elsewhere.

So we are in a much better position. I cringe sometimes when people talk about energy independence in the United States. I think that self-sufficiency is something that we can strive for. Independence would suggest that we are immune to the market, and a disruption anywhere in the world and with everything that is going on geopolitically in the world today in energy-producing countries would have a great impact everywhere around the world, including here. If you look at the crisis in Iraq and what happened in the days after, when the prices spiked around the world, they spiked here in a commensurate way.

So even though our production has increased, we are still susceptible to the market, which still calls for our direct, active leadership and engagement in the world, in the oil markets, and engaging diplomatically with countries that are producing hydrocarbons.

Senator JOHNSON. I appreciate that answer, but what I was really looking for was what happened to the price in Europe when we ended up importing less oil and gas? I actually want some numbers. I am not an oil and gas expert. So I just want to understand what the movement was.

Mr. HOCHSTEIN. Causality is always difficult to address directly, but when the extra volumes from the United States came on the market prices at around the same time came down, from in the $14, $15 range in Europe down to $10 to $12, recently even dipped a little bit lower than that in Europe, the range for natural gas. So that is where you can see the price differential.

Senator JOHNSON. So the current price is about $10?

Mr. HOCHSTEIN. In Europe, it is in that range.

Senator JOHNSON. And in the United States it is . . . ?

Mr. HOCHSTEIN. In the United States today it is, natural gas, $4.30.

Senator JOHNSON. I have heard arguments on both sides, that if we actually export more that would lead toward greater exploration and we would actually build pipelines to capture some of the gas which is flaring, which is wasting. What is your or what is your administration's viewpoint in terms of if we actually did increase more exports; what would actually happen to the price of gas?

Mr. HOCHSTEIN. Well, as far as the administration is concerned, the Department of Energy has approved a fairly large amount of natural gas for export. So I think that tells you what we think about that. There has been some studies——

Senator JOHNSON. No, it really does not.

Mr. HOCHSTEIN. No, I think that we looked at—the Department of Energy commissioned studies and did its own studies on the economic impacts of exports and determined that it would not have— the exports that it has already approved would not have an economic adverse effect on the U.S. price. It could go up some, but it would not have a terribly adverse effect.

Senator JOHNSON. So you basically would be disagreeing with what Senator Markey talks about in terms of dramatically increasing the price of gas if we were to export more?

Mr. HOCHSTEIN. I think if we believed that there would be a dramatic increase in price that we may be more cautious in what we have approved so far in the licenses. But that is why every license that comes, that is submitted for approval, is looked at through that lens of what would be, first of all, the impact on the United States. So far the quantities, which are large, that we have approved, we have not determined to be—would have a detrimental effect.

Senator JOHNSON. In terms of the effect it might have on Vladimir Putin's calculation, even though it would not come on stream immediately, I come from the business world, where I really do believe the customer is king. Customers ought to be more in control of what the pricing levels are versus the supplier. But we have not developed the structure, we have not had the competitive environment, to cause that.

Do you believe that just that signal alone would change or help to change Vladimir Putin's calculation in terms of his long-term control over that marketplace?

Mr. HOCHSTEIN. I believe that Russia and others around the world already have internalized the effects of what the shale gas boom here in the United States has done and that we no longer import the levels that we have, we are going to be a net exporter. I think they have already understood that and that factors in. I think it has had a very important effect.

Senator JOHNSON. Mr. Yee, let me just ask you. I am calling it Putin's pause. I actually appreciate the fact that he has not sent overtly more support and it looks like Ukraine is having some success at stabilizing the region. They are certainly stabilizing some of those cities. Do you have any explanation for that? Do you know what he is thinking?

Mr. YEE. I think it would be very risky to try to get inside Vladimir Putin's brain and to explain what he is thinking.

Senator JOHNSON. Let me just ask: Does that surprise the State Department?

Mr. YEE. That he has paused?

Senator JOHNSON. Yes.

Mr. YEE. I think I would say that it is not a complete surprise in light of some resolve on the part of the international community in standing up to what Russia and Russian proxies are doing in Ukraine, in addition to some bold military action, security action, by the Ukrainian Government and security forces. It should not be a great surprise. We are talking about the recent days.

Since March, I think there has been a cumulative effect with measures led by the United States and NATO in showing that we are absolutely committed first and foremost to our article 5 commitments under the NATO Treaty and putting forces, additional forces, in the front line states near Ukraine, in applying limited sanctions against Russians and Ukrainians who are undermining Ukrainian sovereignty.

I think it is reasonable and it is actually predictable that there would be some pause on——

Senator JOHNSON. What has this administration specifically done to help Ukraine militarily as they are trying to grapple with their security situation?

Mr. YEE. Well, we have, as you know, Senator, a large package of assistance that we have provided to Ukraine, both in terms of assistance to the government in immediate needs for shelter, vehicles, emergency equipment. We have provided nonlethal assistance to the military.

Senator JOHNSON. What does that mean? Specifically what types of equipment have we provided?

Mr. YEE. We are talking about cars, vehicles, basic equipment, nonlethal equipment the military needs in order to perform basic functions. It is nonlethal. It is the type of equipment we feel comfortable at this point providing, and it is what the Ukrainian forces have requested from us.

I am not saying that it is all that is going to be necessary. We are not in any way predicting this is the end, that this pause is somehow the beginning of the end. I think we have to be prepared for a longer effort with continued resolve on the part of not only the United States, but its allies. But we have provided assistance, a large amount of assistance, both in terms of the humanitarian assistance to the people of Ukraine and also assistance in terms of efforts by NATO, the United States and its NATO allies, in putting troops on the ground, putting additional planes in the area, in the front line states, as well as a naval presence in the Black Sea and the Baltic Sea to show that we are determined.

Senator JOHNSON. Thank you.

Thanks, Mr. Chairman.

Senator MURPHY. Thank you both for your testimony. Just one last word on our representation there. Let me just join with Senator Johnson. We need an Ambassador to Romania. This is a country that has great reason to feel imperiled by Russian aggression, and I appreciate some of the work that is being done to make sure that there is a chargé on the ground, but we need an ambassador.

It is also incumbent upon the United States Congress to move on ambassadors that have been named. You mentioned the Czech Republic, for instance, is a country that has paused their plans to build new nuclear technology that is transformational for the Czech Republic, but also potentially for the United States should Westinghouse win that bid. It is really hard for us to represent our Nation's interests if we do not have an ambassador on the ground. We have a chance to confirm a really good one this week, next week, if the Senate acts on that.

So when it comes to making sure that we are fully staffed in embassies, the responsibility is both the administration's to move, I would argue, faster than it has in bringing ambassadors to us and for us to move faster than we have once you bring them to us.

Thank you both for your testimony, and we will sit the second panel now.

[Pause.]

Senator MURPHY. All right. Welcome to our second panel. Senator Johnson is going to return in a few minutes. Let me introduce you briefly, allow you to make brief statements, and then we will get to questions. That was a great first panel, dozens more questions we could have asked, and we will try to direct them to you.

Ambassador Andras Simonyi is the managing director of the Center for Transatlantic Relations at the School of Advanced International Studies at Johns Hopkins. He previously was the

Hungarian Ambassador to the United States and NATO and continues to be an advocate for strong transatlantic relations.

Next to him is Mr. Edward Lucas, a senior fellow and contributing editor at the Center for European Policy Analysis. He is also a senior editor at the Economist, responsible for coverage of energy, commodities, and natural resources. He is one of the foremost experts on Russia and Central and Eastern Europe, having covered that region as a journalist for 25 years, and also wrote a number of very good books on Vladimir Putin, Russia, as well as other topics.

Next to him is Ms. Brenda Shaffer, who is on sabbatical right now from the University of Haifa in Israel, currently a visiting researcher at Georgetown University Center for Eurasian, Russian, and East European Studies. Professor Shaffer is the author of numerous books. She is an expert in the field of energy security policy, Europe, eastern Mediterranean energy issues.

Last but not least, we are very pleased to have with us Edward Chow, a senior fellow in the Energy and National Security Program at the Center for Strategic and International Studies. He has decades of senior-level experience working in the energy industry and has advised the U.S. Government, multinational corporations, and international financial institutions on energy and investment matters. He is widely respected by both sides of the aisle. We are pleased to welcome him back to this committee.

Thank you all for being here. Mr. Ambassador, why do we not start with you. Try to limit your summarized comments to under 5 minutes and then we will just run down the line.

STATEMENT OF AMBASSADOR ANDRAS SIMONYI, MANAGING DIRECTOR, CENTER FOR TRANSATLANTIC RELATIONS, SCHOOL OF ADVANCED INTERNATIONAL STUDIES, JOHNS HOPKINS UNIVERSITY, WASHINGTON, DC

Mr. SIMONYI. Good afternoon. I want to thank you for inviting me here today to discuss this urgent and timely issue. I am honored to be a part of this impressive panel of experts.

Senator Murphy, Senator Johnson, for much too long there has been a disconnect between Europe and the United States when it comes to energy. Most Europeans tend to think of the United States as a country out to destroy the planet and a commonly held view in America is the Europeans are all tree-huggers. Both are extreme and both are wrong and it is in our interests to overcome this divide, the sooner, the better.

The U.S. shale revolution, which has changed the global energy landscape, is an unexpected turn of the last decade. It is a reality, and it is not going away. Europe should have embraced it a long time ago. Europe must put energy security first, as the integrity of its democratic way of life hinges on it.

Lasting and viable solutions cannot be built on ideology. Europe has for too long taken its energy supplies for granted and banked on a breakthrough in renewables and storage technologies which has not happened.

Captains of industry in Europe, like Solvay CEO Jean-Pierre Clamadieu, Exmar CEO Nicolas Saverys, as well as, Gerard Mestrallet, CEO of Gaz de France/Suez were among the first to signal to European leaders the challenges Europe faces with an unrealistic and ideological approach to shale technologies.

European positions are changing. Europe is considerably weakened without a common energy policy. A good sign is the voices of pragmatists in the European Parliament and the European Commission are getting considerably stronger. I agree with Senator Murphy. This movement is way too slow, and Germany is key. I too have a lot of questions about Germany, particularly in which direction Germany is going.

The recent crisis in Ukraine is a huge wake-up call. Russia is using Europe's dependence on supplies to influence European politics and coerce countries into taking positions against transatlantic interests. Since 2009 Europe has been reducing its overall energy dependence on Russia, but for the most vulnerable countries in Central and Eastern Europe, the energy dependence on Russia is a very high 80–90 percent. Energy has become a top security challenge for these countries.

Europe is divided on how to deal with Russia. Russia is actively shaping the European energy debate by influencing organizations and leading public figures and by a sophisticated ''divide and rule'' strategy. There is no consensus on the threats and challenges that Russian policies, in which energy is perhaps the most important tool, pose for the stability of European democracies.

The majority of Europeans hope the United States will continue to see the issue of energy security of its allies as one of its top strategic priorities. The United States is expected to share its gas wealth with Europe. It needs to dispel worries that its energy independence will result in turning away from Europe and from regions on whose security European energy supplies depend.

LNG exports from the United States to Europe would be a strategic message, would strengthen the transatlantic relationship, and besides making economic sense, would create jobs on both sides of the Atlantic. The transatlantic cooperation on energy should result in a more courageous energy mix for Europe that should include all sources, including shale and nuclear.

Europe needs to support the building of interconnectors and port facilities to make U.S. LNG an important factor. In this the U.S. private sector should be actively engaged. We need to use all opportunities to shape a transatlantic energy agenda including through the TTIP—the Transatlantic Trade and Investment Partnership—process, at the forthcoming NATO summit in Cardiff and by reinventing United States-European dialogue and cooperation on energy. The United States and Europe must also lead the international effort on the Future of the Arctic, sometimes a neglected issue.

Finally, the United States and Europe need to get serious on common research on alternatives.

Substantive, practical projects that reinforce transatlantic cooperation could also help to ''de-ideologize'' U.S. and EU approaches to climate change.

I hope Congress will find a way to allow the government to issue LNG export licenses in sufficient numbers for U.S. LNG to make a difference under an Allied Energy Security Act. And while this will not have an immediate impact on European energy security, the political message it would send to Vladimir Putin is incalculable.

And by the way, I hope, Senator Johnson, in the course of the debate you will ask me what I think is in the head of Vladimir Putin when he stopped short of invading the whole of the Ukraine.

What is at stake here, the cohesion and resilience of democratic and free societies, is enormous. And I do feel that the United States must lead. Thank you.

[The prepared statement of Mr. Simonyi follows:]

PREPARED STATEMENT OF ANDRAS SIMONYI

Distinguished members of the subcommittee, Senators Murphy and Johnson, thank you for inviting me to this very timely and important discussion on an issue that cuts to the core of the transatlantic relationship, and which is so important to the security of both the United States and its European allies.

The United States and Europe have been on a different energy trajectory for the past decades. It is an imperative for the United States and its European friends and allies to put their ''ideological'' differences on the back burner, and engage in an effort to align or at least synchronize their energy policies. The recent developments in Ukraine and the ever-increasing efforts by Russia to wield its energy weapon is a wake-up call.

Europe, roughly speaking, has embraced a radical ''ideological'' view on climate change and fossil fuels, banking on a breakthrough in renewables technologies. The breakthrough has not happened. Europe's dependence on Russian gas has increased. There is no common European energy policy, which is a prerequisite of the alignment of, or at least synchronization of energy policies of the EU and the United States. European captains of industry, like Solvay Chairman Jean Pierre Clamadieu, and some member state governments of the EU, were sounding the alarm well before the Ukraine crisis, calling for a better energy mix, which should include traditional sources of fossil fuels and coal, but also nuclear and shale gas. In the past few months, there are signs of a more pragmatic approach within the European Commission, the administrative body of the European Union.

Over the last 5 years the United States has gone through an energy revolution, with energy independence becoming a reality in the very near future. This has been an unexpected change of fortune for America. For decades the United States and EU have been dependent on fossil fuel resources from OPEC and Russia. Now this formula has been turned on its head by transformational U.S. energy developments generated in particular by a surge in production of cheap natural gas and shale oil.

Yet as U.S. prospects brighten and foreign dependence falls, Europe's energy picture has become muddled and its dependence is rising. These developments are likely to have profound yet still uncertain implications for U.S.-European relations; they require greater transatlantic attention.

It is an imperative for the United States and Europe (meaning the European Union and the European Free Trade Association) to put their ''ideological'' differences on the back burner, and engage in an effort to align or at least synchronize their energy policies.

The United States is and remains Europe's most important strategic and economic partner. It is clearly in the interests of the United States work as closely as possible with Europe on the future of transatlantic energy and to do what it can to make Europe less energy dependent on Russia, while understanding that Russia will remain a key source of Europe's energy. Steps by the United States to allow for generous issuing of export licenses to Europe would be important, strategic decisions that would have a long-term economic impact, improve supply diversity, and—perhaps equally important—have an immediate political impact.

At the same time Europe must be courageous and embrace a common energy strategy that allows for diverse solutions. The European Commission, in its latest recommendation, encourages a radical embrace of the energy mix, not excluding shale or nuclear. The EU must also take further steps to de-ideologize its internal debate, not forcing a choice between a sound energy policy and a sound climate policy, but finding a balance to accommodate both, but with a lot more realism. There are signs that the debate is changing, as recently as last week Germany decided to allow the ''exploration of the possibilities of shale gas.'' However, time is of the essence, and Europe needs to move fast.

28

FRAMING THE ISSUES

A number of issues deserve attention. First are basic issues of relative competitiveness. How is growing U.S. energy production likely to interact with declining EU production and growing EU reliance on outside sources in terms of price differentials, relative dependencies, energy mix, and basic economic fundamentals? How might such differentials translate into changes in trade and investment patterns? What sectors are most likely to be affected?

Second, Americans and Europeans still tend to talk past each other when it comes to issues of energy and climate. At times it seems to be a "clash of religions": Americans tend to believe that European preoccupation with their image as the "champion" of climate issues has blinded them to key dependencies and the need for a clear and common energy policy. Europeans tend to believe that American preoccupation with the notion of energy independence has blinded them to the dangers posed by a changing climate and caused them to pull back from vigorous efforts to develop breakthrough energy solutions. Neither view is entirely true, but these differing perceptions have contributed to a dialogue of the deaf that often finds the United States and the EU in opposing camps globally. That is in the interest of neither partner. How may changing energy dynamics alter such approaches? Is there room for greater transatlantic alignment?

Third, there is a growing transatlantic foreign policy disconnect when it comes to the implications of diverging U.S. and European energy trajectories. Are America's changing energy dependencies resulting in reduced U.S. interest in engaging with allies or retrenchment from traditional regions of U.S. foreign policy concern? Could there be a new transatlantic strategic bargain involving energy and security elements? Can energy become a common denominator for common interests and values in a new world, or are evolving energy dynamics more likely to pull Europeans and Americans further apart?

KEY DEVELOPMENTS

Changing energy dynamics have generated a host of geostrategically relevant trends.

The geopolitics of energy itself has been transformed. For more than 30 years America and Europe lived in a world in which 80 percent of fossil fuel resources were in the hands of OPEC and Russia and only 10 percent in the hands of OECD countries and China. With shale being dispersed worldwide the 80:10 ratio has imploded.

The impact, however, is uneven. Major petro-states such as the Russian Federation and Saudi Arabia need high oil prices to fund budgets to keep their restive populations passive. The shale revolution challenges their approaches. For Europe there is potential for long-term gain, but it is being overshadowed by short-term pain. And despite the energy revolution, global energy demand is still likely to double by 2050. Uneven access to energy could exacerbate disparities between energy haves and have-nots, with implications for Western security and prosperity.

By mid-century the strategic centrality of the Middle East in the global supply of hydrocarbons in their present form may well have been lost in the new context of global shale gas and tight oil production. Conventional hydrocarbon production in the Middle East, however, will still play an important role in determining global supply, and to the extent that this continues, the U.S. and other powers will continue to project power in the region. Some U.S. allies and the global economy more broadly will continue to be dependent on energy reserves controlled by problematic regimes, even if the U.S. is not. But the relative attention and roles of various actors are likely to change over time.

The full implications for the United States are also unclear. While fashionable notions of U.S. decline seem impossible to sustain in the face of surging U.S. energy production, the 1973 oil crisis occurred when the United States was dependent upon foreign sources of oil and gas for only about 15 percent of its energy demands, and the United States is likely to be more dependent on hydrocarbon imports than this for at least the next decade.

Moreover, many U.S. partners wonder whether the new energy dynamics could interact with other trends to weaken their relationship with Washington. Some Arab leaders already think that the oil-for-security deal in the Middle East is fading because they perceive that America's energy revolution has made Washington less interested in that bargain. These perceptions have already had an impact on U.S. engagement in the region.

Europeans are also increasingly concerned about U.S. retrenchment due to energy dynamics, as well as other trends. There is widespread uncertainty in Europe about the U.S. commitment to the transatlantic relationship in general and U.S. interest in European energy security in particular. The "pivot toward Asia," and the widely used expression "U.S. energy independence," have been interpreted as signs that the United States continues to flirt with unilateralism at the expense of engagement with allies. There is growing concern that previous U.S. efforts to facilitate the development of new pipelines in Turkey, the Caucasus and Central Asia, and to lower European energy reliance on Russia and the Middle East, are no longer important as the United States grows more self-reliant. These developments render it even harder to find transatlantic common ground on energy security.

Taken together, these developments underscore the need for policies that are proactive rather than reactive. Today's world of haves and have-nots, asymmetric challenges and diffusion of power offers policymakers less time and less order to make decisions, and large institutions are often ill-equipped to adjust to the speed of change. Prevention of conflict has become as important as reaction to conflict. The ability to shape the environment in which countries develop, and to help frame decisions that leaders and populations make, remains as relevant as the ability to command or compel change.

In short, energy is front and center on the strategic agenda. It is a transformational issue and must be addressed as such.

EUROPE'S CHALLENGES

The crisis in Ukraine has highlighted the seriousness of the role of Russia in Europe's energy supplies. The divisions and the reactions to the Russian annexation of Ukraine have been highly influenced by the levels of importance of Russia's relative significance as a given country's gas supplier. This link is also apparent in the attitudes of certain EU members toward sanctions.

The challenge posed by Russia to Europe, has been in the making for a long time. Some of the newest members of the alliance (Hungary, Slovakia, Czech Republic, the Baltics, Bulgaria and Croatia) are among the most vulnerable. Perhaps it is not an exaggeration to suggest that Europe has been naive about the relationship being one of interdependence. Russia provides approximately one-third of Europe's overall gas supplies, but for some countries of Central and Eastern Europe, the economically and politically most vulnerable part of Europe, it is up to 80–90 percent in some cases. The building of the North and South Stream pipelines and the abandoning of the Nabucco project have made the Russian hold on Europe stronger. The European Commission has made laudable efforts to reign in Gazprom's monopolistic practices, but Europe needs a clearer strategy to find alternative sources, to be able to resist Russian pressures.

KEY PROBLEMS OF THE EUROPEAN ENERGY ECONOMY

EU energy vulnerability is growing. The EU faces a future of limited domestic fossil fuel production from conventional resources as the North Sea begins to deplete. In fact, as the shale revolution takes hold worldwide Europe becomes on current policies the only major economic bloc without access to domestic fossil fuel resources at scale. Varying EU approaches to nuclear energy have contributed to this vulnerability. Europe also remains dependent on three principal external suppliers of conventional energy: Algeria, Russia, and Norway. Various Central and Eastern Europe countries—members of both the EU and NATO—are particularly concerned about their energy dependency on Russia. The failure of Nabucco and the delivery of a small amount of gas by the end of the decade (probably at most 10bcm) via the Trans-Adriatic Pipeline does not bode well for new alternative gas sources into Europe. There is the prospect of gas from the Eastern Mediterranean toward the end of the decade. However, the capital has be found, local geopolitics addressed and the resources extracted and transported. None of these factors are yet secure. Moreover, the stresses caused by the shale revolution on Saudi Arabia and the Russian Federation could render Europe's immediate eastern and southeastern neighborhood more unstable.

There appears to be little chance of significant shale production in Europe, even if efforts go forward. There is no indigenous industry of this type or a finance market that can securitize loans for drilling rigs; deposits are far deeper and thus harder to develop than deposits identified in many other world regions; and property laws limit incentives and opportunities, as do widespread environmental concerns and Europe's population density. The more immediate impact of shale on Europe is less likely to come from fracking directly in Europe than from fracking elsewhere—particularly the United States. But if countries such as China or Australia also engage in large-scale fracking it could free up gas from Qatar and other suppliers.

30

Europe has also been hit with a triple-whammy of higher energy costs due to climate change policies, natural gas prices linked to oil, and low U.S. natural gas prices stemming from its shale revolution. Between 2005 and 2012 gas prices for industry fell by 66 percent in America but rose 35 percent in Europe, according to the European Commission. One result is that a significant number of energy-intensive European companies are considering relocation to the United States, where industrial gas prices are about one-quarter those in Europe.

EU climate change policies have largely failed to reduce CO_2 emissions, despite extensive EU and member state regulatory structures and renewables subsidies. The focus has been on cutting carbon emission production rather than consumption (with the exception of a few countries, notably the Nordics), and carbon-based imports are simply replacing what is no longer produced in Europe.

One effect has been to encourage greater use of cheap coal to offset the cost of renewables. America's shale-gas bonanza has displaced to Europe coal that had previously been burned in America, pushing European coal prices down relative to gas prices. At the same time carbon prices crashed because there were too many permits to emit carbon in Europe's emissions-trading system and the recession cut demand for them. This has reduced penalties for burning coal and kept profit margins for coal-fired power plants healthy while slashing profit margins for gas-fired plants. In Germany, for instance, carbon emissions have gone up, not down; production of brown coal electricity is at its highest levels since 1990; and the country has become America's largest global customer of coal.

Many European opinion leaders are still in a state of shock, and many in denial, about the nature of their dependence, their policy misfortunes, and the implications of the global shale revolution. European leaders once thought that they were leading the way toward the era of low-carbon power. The original EU climate strategy was motivated as much by competitive thinking as it was by concern for the environment. The prevailing notion at the time was that the EU's ability to break through to a hyper-energy-efficient model in a high fossil-fuel-price world would generate competitive advantage for the EU vis-a-vis its energy-guzzling competitors. Yet in austerity conditions the 20/20/20 program imposed significant costs on EU member states, and the new energy environment has rendered questionable the price calculations that underpinned Europe's renewables revolution.

The Ukraine crisis has prompted a quick regional response from central Europe, from the Baltic States and from the Nordic countries as well. There is a realization that diversifying sources of supply is only one element in the process of increasing energy independence. New interconnectors are being built, regional cooperation enhanced, further ways to increase energy efficiency are being explored.

As a result, the EU has an integrated climate change policy yet no integrated energy policy. Liberalization of Europe's gas markets would force Gazprom and other giants to open their pipelines to competitors, and would bring down prices. The European Commission estimates that fully integrated gas and electricity markets could yield savings of up to 65 billion euros [86 billion dollars] annually.

Some progress has been made. There are now much deeper liquid gas markets across the continent. Around half of gas is now traded on hubs. Interconnections are being put in place and the European Commission's antitrust arm is bearing down on Gazprom. Nonetheless, European energy policies remain fragmented, with many countries going their own way.

A NEW STRATEGIC BARGAIN

Senator Murphy, Senator Johnson, aligning U.S. and European energy policies is of renewed strategic importance, as key energy producing regions become more volatile and new energy producers and sources emerge, as the United States debates its shale boom and the potential for energy exports to Europe, and as the United States and the EU negotiate a potentially transformative Transatlantic Trade and Investment Partnership (TTIP). Stakeholders in government and parliaments, energy producers and consumers, energy-intensive sectors, experts and other opinion leaders need to establish a new path for dialogue across the Atlantic.

Unfortunately, current transatlantic mechanisms are broken. A formal U.S.-EU Transatlantic Energy Council and other venues exist, but their effectiveness is questionable. Each transatlantic partner is setting its own priorities with inadequate regard for the other.

Much of the transatlantic debate, of course, is likely to be influenced by how each side of the Atlantic addresses its own domestic issues—whether the United States changes current market distortions and bans on oil and gas exports; whether the EU can create a single energy market or change prevailing approaches premised on high energy prices; or whether either can escape the lingering effects of the Great Recession.

There is potential, however, for a new strategic bargain based on a problem-solving approach using energy dynamics to help address various geostrategic challenges.

Both the cold war and post-cold-war models of transatlantic security partnership seem less attuned to today's challenges. While Washington has signaled its continued commitment to the alliance, it argues that it is not unreasonable to expect European allies to step up their relative contributions and engagement. The U.S. has demonstrated that it is prepared to provide assets only it has—whether political credibility in Kosovo; cruise missiles in Libya; or advanced communications and logistics capacities in Mali—but it has made it clear that it does not need to command every operation and expects European allies and partners to bear the brunt of the burden for managing regional crises below the threshold of mutual self-defense.

U.S. leaders look to progress in Europe's efforts to enhance its capabilities as the most visible measure of its commitment to a fuller partnership in maintaining transatlantic and global security. So far they have been disappointed. Yet if the United States would add energy to the mix, there is a reasonable chance that Europe may respond.

A strategic initiative of this type would be more than a crude energy-for-security deal. But at its core the United States would signal willingness to work energetically on an energy partnership with Europe, including U.S. exports, and European partners would signal a willingness to step up their geopolitical engagement in regions abutting Europe and engage in more proactive efforts to address a range of geopolitical challenges, many far from European shores. This strategic package might usefully consist of various elements, including the following.

An Allied Energy Security Act (AESA), under which the U.S. Congress would fast track waivers of Department of Energy export licensing for up to 100bcm of natural gas to NATO allies or member states of the European Union. Above 100bcm the normal export licensing process would apply. The AESA would also permit the White House to seek further waivers from DOE procedures from the Senate should a "grave supply situation" arise that could threaten the security of its allies. This would be similar to national security exemptions, currently in place, which allow the U.S. administration to take action that might otherwise be in violation of certain regulations. At my last count 6 export applications have been approved and 24 are awaiting action, although this may have changed recently. The approval of AESA would be important for commitments by U.S. companies to invest in European LNG capabilities.

In parallel with the AESA, NATO allies and EU member states would commit to enhance their responsibility for Western energy security in the Mediterranean and the gulf. This would mean at a minimum that France and the United Kingdom would have to be willing to maintain substantial naval forces in the region, potentially taking over from the U.S. Fifth Fleet in Bahrain.

These efforts would be buttressed by those of the NATO Alliance itself. Allies have already agreed that NATO has a legitimate role to play regarding energy security. As the alliance's major operational focus on Afghanistan winds down, there may be more policy space for greater NATO attention to energy issues. For instance, as part of an expanded and realistic plan for NATO partnership with North Africa, NATO countries could support and advise Libya and Algeria on pipeline security and oil fields and help them create a secure platform for continued production and investment in fossil fuel facilities, including Algeria's rich shale resources. NATO could even take a lead across the Mediterranean basin to reinforce supply security for all states in the region. This could include training, exercises, and education to help protect the states from terrorist attacks, threats of supply cut off and technical threats to supply. This would also include cooperation with the member states in maintaining energy security in the EU and the European neighborhood. It would include technical security of pipelines and energy facilities as well as a broader range of measures to support EU and regional action.

Energy should become a key element of the negotiations on the Transatlantic Trade and Investment Partnership (TTIP). More effective energy cooperation was not an original impetus for the talks, but should now be incorporated to facilitate U.S. energy exports to Europe, align standards in areas such as e-mobility and energy efficiency, reduce tariff and nontariff barriers to clean energy goods and services, and create mechanisms for mutual recognition of regulatory processes regarding energy innovation. In essence, members of the TTIP and the Trans-Pacific Partnership alike should be eligible for waivers to DOE licensing requirements.

The United States and its European partners must reengage strategically on Wider Europe. Twenty years after the European revolutions of 1989, much of

Europe has integrated. But the unsettled spaces of Wider Europe are significantly less democratic, less secure, and less aligned with the West than some years ago. Russia's forceful annexation of the Crimean region of Ukraine, and its active support for armed separatists in other Ukrainian regions, are the most dramatic but by no means the only examples of this challenge. The U.S. and its European allies should reengage to help stop backsliding and to project stability. Successes in this region—secure energy production and transit, more effective democratic governance grounded in the rule of law, progress against corruption and trafficking, peaceful resolution of conflicts, more confident and prosperous market economies—could resonate significantly across the post-Soviet space and into the broader Middle East, and enhance the region's potential as a strategic bridge. Failure to deal with the region's problems risks dysfunctional energy markets, destabilizing competition and confrontation among both regional and external actors, festering separatist conflicts, and greater transnational challenges, the negative consequences of which could spill over into Europe, Eurasia, and the Middle East. While much progress depends primarily on the people of the region, much also depends on the nations of the West.

The next 2–3 years are critical for setting out the long-term patterns of managing the future development of the Arctic region. As Arctic ice melts, Arctic states and other major economic powers, such as Japan and China, are increasing efforts to exploit energy resources and fisheries, open shipping routes, and variously reinforce a commercial, military and coastal security presence. All this is taking place across the backdrop of a fragile geophysical environment already degraded in many areas and disproportionately subject to the effects of global warming. The United States and its North American and European partners need to set forth a comprehensive approach to the Arctic, backed at high level, to address key interests and prevent potential future crises before the melting ice brings differing national agendas into conflict.

Energy discoveries in the Eastern Mediterranean could offer the transatlantic partners a way to clear the many blockages in the region, including the Cyprus problem, to create a basis for significant offshore development.

There is significant potential for more effective U.S.-EU efforts in energy research and development. Joint efforts to advance clean coal technologies and carbon capture, storage and sequestration could not only benefit the transatlantic partners; China and India will continue to use coal, so changes to coal production techniques could have significant global impact. Aligning standards on safe nuclear energy would also lift global standards. Consideration might be given to a U.S.-EU Clean Energy Bank and Transatlantic Energy Innovation Fund. The Clean Energy Bank, which would be open to others, would underwrite the risks of developing new, commercially viable technologies. It would help commercialize new technologies, some of which might be developed under the Innovation Fund. That fund would support joint research and development to accelerate the introduction of new technologies for electric mobility (car technology, batteries, infrastructure); super smart grid; renewable energy development and deployment; carbon capture and storage; and energy efficiency. Such agreements would allow the EU and United States to pool scarce research resources, encourage faster and broader roll out of new technologies, and rapidly develop common standards for new technologies for further dissemination.

Substantive, practical projects that reinforce transatlantic cooperation could also help to "de-ideologize" U.S. and EU approaches to climate change. Multilateral climate discussions have essentially become donors' conferences. It is essential to transform them into a more robust platform for engagement on related issues of economic and technological development and trade. The chances of that happening are higher if the United States and the EU align their approaches.

EU–U.S. energy cooperation would be further enhanced through greater attention to the Energy Renaissance that is occurring across the entire Atlantic Basin. Over the next 20 years the Atlantic is likely to become the energy reservoir of the world and a net exporter of many forms of energy to the Indian Ocean and Pacific Ocean Basins. The Atlantic is setting the global pace for energy innovation and redrawing global maps for oil, gas, and renewables as new players and technologies emerge, new conventional and unconventional sources come online, energy services boom, and opportunities appear all along the energy supply chain. Together these developments are shifting the center of gravity for global energy supply from the Middle East to the Atlantic Hemisphere.

Our Center at Johns Hopkins SAIS is coordinating an Atlantic Basin Initiative to advance this new agenda. Leading private and public sector leaders from all four Atlantic continents will meet this November in Mexico at the inaugural Atlantic Energy Forum under our auspices to consider ways to facilitate and develop Atlantic Basin energy trade and investment; remove barriers; eliminate illicit energy trade;

enable best possible access to capital, further development and interconnection of energy transport infrastructure; improve energy access and reduce energy poverty; and promote energy mixes designed to minimize negative environmental consequences in cost-effective ways.

Allow me as a final point to stress that in my view the United States should take the lead on a strategic debate on energy security in the transatlantic community. For this the forthcoming NATO summit must task the North Atlantic Council to regularly discuss the issue and make recommendations relevant to the alliance as a whole, or to individual member states. NATO needs to monitor national policies from a security standpoint.

Senator MURPHY. Thank you.
Mr. Lucas.

STATEMENT OF EDWARD LUCAS, SENIOR FELLOW AND CONTRIBUTING EDITOR, CENTER FOR EUROPEAN POLICY ANALYSIS, WASHINGTON, DC

Mr. LUCAS. Good afternoon and thank you for inviting me. It is an honor and a privilege for a European to be invited here to talk. I have got some written testimony which I shall just summarize briefly. I would like to thank Chairman Murphy and Ranking Member Johnson for the opportunity.

European security really matters to the United States. Europe is your largest trading partner and Europe is a force multiplier. It is your most important ally. And Europe is under attack. It is under attack from Vladimir Putin's Russia in ways that we have not completely understood, because we tend to compartmentalize things. We think this is an energy problem, this is a military problem, this is a diplomatic problem. In Putin's Russia all these things mix together. You have business, statecraft, intelligence, organized crime, energy, military force, all overlapping and interlocking.

As you referred to in your opening remarks, Russia is a revisionist power and I think we have understood that Russia is trying to tear up the European security order. That is what it did with its invasion of Crimea. It is perhaps less understood that Russia is also trying to tear up the European energy order. It regards to EU's ability to be the rule-setter in European energy as an existential threat, because Vladimir Putin's power at home and abroad depends on the abuse of energy markets, particularly through the way he manipulates gas exports. And the European Union has been doing a pretty good job to stop that, as we have heard, with the Third Energy Package, with the growth of interconnectors and storage and things like that.

And Putin does not like that. As you saw in your visit to Bulgaria, he is very keen to push ahead with South Stream, which is an absolute head-on challenge to the European energy order, and he has managed to get six EU countries now lined up in support of South Stream, and that is pretty bad.

So this revisionism affects more than just the conventional military thing. Russia has got the means to be revisionist. I think we are still sometimes mentally in the 1990s, where Russia is a poor country. Even now, people say Russia is a declining country. Well, maybe it is a declining country, but it can still do us an awful lot of damage.

It is not just the military buildup that we have seen, and the willingness to use force, which gives it an edge over European countries, who basically do not want to. It has been able to use the energy weapon over a period of years to constrain Europe's decisionmaking ability. European countries that worry about their supplies of Russian natural gas do not want to offend Russia. They feel vulnerable.

It has also used the money that spins off from energy and from other things to foster very powerful lobbies—commercial, financial, economic lobbies—of people who have got a direct business interest in having good political relations with Russia. We see this in Germany, the Netherlands, particularly, I am sorry to say, in my own country, Britain, where the city of London is perhaps the biggest laundry machine for Russian money, and there is a very strong political pushback in Britain when we try and do things that might offend the Russian Government.

I should also mention information warfare, which is something that we have neglected. I am happy to go into that in the Q and A. Russia practices information warfare against the West with a sophistication and intensity that we did not even see during the cold war. They are using techniques of social media, using YouTube, using all sorts of other things against us, and we do not really have an answer. And of course they are also willing to use force.

I think we also have to acknowledge and agree that Russia is winning. Regardless of whether there is a pause in Ukraine or not, the fact is they got away with it. They got away with the Crimea and they are getting away with it in the pushback on energy. A particularly good example of that is that the EU has put on hold what would have been potentially a devastating response to Russia, which is the complaint against Gazprom.

If anyone had told Mr. Putin in 2005, 2006, 2007, 2008 that EU officials with search warrants would be kicking down doors and going to Gazprom affiliates all over Europe, seizing documents, seizing computers, and building up a compelling picture of market abuse that could lead to hundreds of millions of dollars in fines on Gazprom, enormous legally mandated changes to their business model, and possibly class action law suits—we do not know what goes on inside Putin's head, but it would not have been pretty.

That is what happened. The EU got to the stage where it had a loaded weapon pointed at the Kremlin and then it flinched in pulling the trigger.

We need to do all sorts of things. We need to deal with the military dimension, particularly a standing defense plan for the Baltics, prepositioning, all that sort of stuff. We need to send a message that crime does not pay. We need to do the Magnitsky sanctions on a much wider scale.

I think American LNG is a vital part of the picture and I am very glad that you touched on that. Even before a molecule of LNG arrived in Lithuania, thanks to Lithuania's LNG terminal, which has not actually been delivered yet, they were able to drive a much harder bargain with Gazprom and get a much lower gas price. So I think one has to see LNG and LNG infrastructure not just in business terms, but in national security terms, and from that point of view it is vital for Europe, and the American export licenses already granted play a very important psychological component in that, even before any molecules flow.

Finally, I would just touch on energy market reform. Russia habitually abuses the energy market. It abuses the setting of benchmarks. Its trading companies abuse the market. A lot of this stuff is very difficult to write about publicly because of English libel laws, and I refer in my written testimony to my coordinating The Economist's libel defense when we were sued by someone who is now on the U.S. sanctions list.

This really deserves the full attention of the American criminal justice system. You have all sorts of evidence about money-laundering, market abuse, insider trading, and all sorts of other stuff that goes on. You have the ability to clean this up, and the more open, the more transparent, the more liquid world energy markets are, the better everybody else is and the safer Europe will be.

I will stop there.

[The prepared statement of Mr. Lucas follows:]

PREPARED STATEMENT OF EDWARD LUCAS

Good afternoon. Thank you for inviting me here today. It is an honor and a privilege to give testimony to this committee and I would like to thank Chairman Murphy and Ranking Member Johnson for this opportunity. I will give a short oral version of my written testimony and then look forward to taking questions.

I have been dealing with European security for more than 30 years, as an activist for freedom and democracy during the cold war, as a foreign correspondent and editor for major international media outlets, and also as a senior nonresident fellow at the Centre for European Policy Analysis—CEPA—here in DC. I speak Russian, German, Polish, Czech, and some other languages.

In 1989 I was the only foreign newspaperman living in Communist-era Czechoslovakia and witnessed the Velvet Revolution bring down that regime. I was the last Western journalist to be expelled from the Soviet Union, for having crossed the border with the first visa given by the new but unrecognised Lithuanian authorities. In 1992 I founded and ran the first English-language weekly in the Baltic States. In 2010 I coordinated the defence for my employer, The Economist, in a high-stakes libel action brought against us by Gennady Timchenko, a Russian energy tycoon who denied our claim that had benefited from his association with Vladimir Putin.

I am the author of two books on the regime in Russia. The first of these, "The New Cold War," was written in 2007, at a time when most Westerners were still reluctant to face up to the threat the regime poses both to its own people, and to Russia's neighbours. Many accused me of scaremongering. Few do that now.

Yet conventional thinking about Russia has surprisingly deep roots. Many people in Washington, Brussels, London, and Berlin believe that Vladimir Putin's Russia can be accommodated diplomatically. Money doesn't smell. Energy is just a business. There is no need to take radical measures in response to the latest crisis in Ukraine. The danger is of a provocative over-reaction, not of appeasement.

I disagree profoundly. My views are based on my experiences over many years in in Estonia, Latvia, Lithuania, Poland, the Czech Republic, Russia, and other countries in the region. People there have been warning us for years of the dangerous direction of events. We have not listened to them. Instead, we have systematically patronised, belittled, and ignored those who know the problem better than we do. Now they have been proved right. I hope that my voice may be heard, where theirs, still, is not.

My first point is that Russia is a revisionist power. The Kremlin not only regards the existing European security order as unfair but actively seeks to change it. It wants to weaken the Atlantic alliance, to divide NATO, and to undermine the European Union's role as a rule-setter, especially in energy policy. On issues such as the South Stream pipeline, access to gas storage, reverse flow and other issues the unsung bureaucrats of the EU Commission represent an existential threat to the Kremlin's business model.

Russia begrudges the former captive nations of the Soviet empire their freedom, their prosperity, and particularly their independence. It maintains an old-fashioned idea of "legitimate interests" and "spheres of influence" in which the future geopolitical orientation of countries such as Ukraine and Georgia is not a matter of sovereign choice for the peoples of those nations, but a question in which Russia has, by right, a veto.

My second point is that Russia, a leading petrostate, now has the means to pursue its revisionist approach:

- It ruthlessly uses its energy weapon against European countries, particularly in pipeline-delivered gas, where it has a substantial monopoly in the eastern half of the continent.
- It uses money. It bolsters a self-interested commercial and financial lobby which profits from doing business with Russia and fears any cooling in political relations. Austrian banks, German industrial exporters, French defence contractors, and a slew of companies, banks, and law firms in my own country, the United Kingdom, exemplify this. These energy and financial ties constrain the Western response to Russian revisionism.
- It practises information warfare (propaganda) with a level of sophistication and intensity not seen even during the cold war. This confuses and corrodes Western decisionmaking abilities.
- It is prepared to threaten and use force.

My third point is that Russia is winning. Too much attention is paid to the ebb and flow of events in Ukraine. The big picture is bleak: Russia has successfully challenged the European security order. It has seized another country's territory, fomented insurrection, and engaged in repeated acts of military saber-rattling, subversion and economic coercion. The response from the West has been weak and disunited. The United States is distracted by multiple urgent problems elsewhere. You rightly wonder why you should be bearing the cost of increasing European security. For their part many European countries have no appetite for confrontation with Russia.

My fourth point is that greater dangers lie ahead. Russia has mounted a bold defence of its market-abusing South Stream pipeline, signing up Austria, Hungary, Croatia, Slovenia, Bulgaria, and Greece in support of a direct challenge to the EU's rules on pipeline construction and third-party access. The Ukrainian adventure has given a big boost to the Putin regime in Russia, which had previously shown some signs of declining popularity, amid economic failure and growing discontent about corruption and poor public services. The big danger is that as the effect of seizing Crimea wears off (and as the costs of doing so bear more heavily on Russia's sagging finances), the regime is tempted to try something else.

Our weakness over Ukraine makes that more likely. We have set the stage for another, probably more serious challenge to European security, most likely in the Baltic States. Estonia, Latvia, and Lithuania are loyal American allies and NATO members. If any one of them is successfully attacked or humiliated, NATO will lose its credibility overnight, permanently and irreversibly. These are our frontline states: the safety and security that we have taken for granted since the end of the cold war now hangs on their fate.

But geography is against them: the Baltic States form a thin, flat strip of land, lightly populated and with no natural frontier and little strategic depth. Russia knows that. NATO has only a token presence in the region. We have no hardened infrastructure, no prepositioned military forces, weapons or munitions. Russia knows that too. Their economies are liable to Russian pressure (especially in natural gas, where they are 100 percent dependent on Russian supplies). Estonia and Latvia are also vulnerable to Russian interference because of their ethnic makeup (between a quarter and a third of their populations self-identify as "Russian" in some sense).

What can we do?

The first task is to see clearly what has happened. European security will not be fixed with a few deft diplomatic touches. To cope with a revisionist Russia it needs a fundamental overhaul. American and European policymakers need to explain to the public that the war in Ukraine was a game-changer.

We need to rebut the phoney Realpolitik arguments, which advise us to make the best of a bad job. We should accept the loss of Crimea, so the argument goes, do a deal with Russia over the future of Ukraine, and get used to the new realities, of a Russian droit de regard in neighbouring countries.

Such an approach would be morally wrong and strategically stupid.

Securing a Europe whole and free after 1991 has been a magnificent achievement in which the United States has played a huge part. True: we made mistakes. We declared "job done" in 2004, when 10 ex-Communist countries joined NATO. That was far too early. We overlooked Russian resentment at the way Europe was evolving, and our vulnerability to Russian pushback. We neglected Ukraine, Moldova, Belarus, and the countries of the Caucasus. But having made these mistakes is no reason to compound them now, by retreating into a grubby defeatism. To go back to business as usual would send a message that the kleptocratic regime in the Kremlin would understand all too well: crime pays.

Legitimising Russia's land-grab in Ukraine, and its attempted power-grab in the wider neighbourhood, would also fly in the face of historical justice. The Crimean Tatars—whose suffering at Soviet hands is all but unmatched—are now under the rule of their former tormentors. Are we really proposing that whole countries, which the past masters of the Kremlin occupied and despoiled, should be subject to renewed interference and manipulation?

Instead, we should make it clear that we will boost our allies and weaken our opponents. We do not want to be enemies with Russia. But if the Putin regime treats us as an enemy, we help nobody by pretending otherwise.

The most immediate priority is military. A security crisis in the Baltic region is the single most dangerous threat facing the Atlantic alliance. Reckless behaviour by Russia could face us with a choice between a full-scale military confrontation (including the potential use of nuclear weapons) or surrender, with the collapse of our most fundamental security arrangements. We must make every effort to ensure that this does not happen.

That means American and other allies prepositioning military equipment and supplies in the Baltic States. It means NATO creating a standing defence plan—one which assumes that there is a real and present danger of attack. We need to put a major NATO base in Poland, to reassure that country that it can safely deploy its forces to the Baltics as reinforcements in the event of a crisis. We need to boost the NATO presence in the Baltic States with rotating visits by naval vessels, extended air-policing, and ground forces—initially on persistent rotation, but as soon as possible on permanent deployment.

Russia will complain vigorously about this. But the fact that the Kremlin is unhappy when its neighbours are secure is telling. We should explain to the Russian authorities that when NATO expanded in 2004, we did not even draw up contingency plans for the military defence of the new members, because we assumed that Russia was a friend, not a threat. It is Russia's behaviour which has changed that. Russia attacked Georgia in 2008. It rehearsed the invasion and occupation of the Baltic States a year later, in the Zapad-09 exercise (which concluded with a dummy nuclear strike on Warsaw). It has continued to menace the Baltic States ever since, with air-space violations, propaganda and economic warfare, and state-sponsored subversion. We take the step of securing our most vulnerable allies belatedly and reluctantly, and solely as a result of Russian policy directed toward them.

A further vital military component of security in north-eastern Europe is the closest possible integration of Sweden and Finland into NATO planning and capabilities. These countries are not members of the alliance, so they cannot formally be part of its command structure. But we should make every effort to maximise cooperation in every respect. We cannot defend the Baltic States or Poland without their help. It is commendable that the United States is selling the JASMM missile to Finland. It should continue the further sale of advanced precision and stealth weaponry on a wide scale to both countries. NATO's summit in Wales this fall, which will have little to offer on expansion, should make a point of offering a "gold card" partnership to Sweden and Finland. The United States should take every opportunity to foster high-level political dialogue with both countries in and around NATO. Rich, well-run countries with serious military capabilities, excellent intelligence services and strong strategic cultures are in short supply in modern Europe. We should make the most of what we have.

The United States should also continue to make good on its promises of missile defence installations in the region. The administration should also consider the interim deployment of armed Patriot missiles in Poland—a promise which the Polish Government believes was solemnly made by the George W. Bush administration, but never honoured.

Having shored up our most vulnerable allies, the next task is stabilising Ukraine. It is hard to overstate how parlous the situation is. How much more Ukrainian territory ends up under direct or indirect Russian control is of secondary importance. Ukraine is going to be in the political and economic emergency room for years to come. That is Russia's doing. Ukraine is suffering a world-class economic and financial crisis, which even in a stable and secure country would be far worse than anything experienced elsewhere in Europe. The economy is fundamentally uncompetitive. The main export market, Russia, is at risk of closure at any moment. Public finances are in ruins. The government subsists on a hand-to-mouth basis, relying on ad-hoc donations from wealthy oligarchs for even core spending requirements such as national defence. Even if everything else goes well, simply fixing Ukraine's economy will take 5 years.

The outside world must respond generously and imaginatively. A new Marshall Plan for Ukraine should involve not only direct financial support, but the widest possible relaxation of tariffs and quotas on Ukrainian products such as steel, grain, textiles, and agricultural products. The European Union has led the way with the newly signed deep and comprehensive free trade agreement, but much more remains to be done. In particular, European countries should accelerate efforts to supply Ukraine with natural gas by reversing the flow of existing pipelines. Russia has already threatened unspecified sanctions against countries which re-export Russian gas—a sign of how seriously the Kremlin treats the issue.

Second, Ukraine faces a political and constitutional crisis of a kind unseen since the end of the wars in ex-Yugoslavia. Every political institution was degraded and discredited under the previous Yanukovych regime. Decades of bad government, corruption and abysmal public services have corroded public confidence in the state—one reason for the initial public support enjoyed by the insurgents in the poorest parts of eastern Ukraine. The United States should press for early parliamentary elections, and offer support for institution-building, and especially the vexed question of relations between the center and the regions.

Third, Ukraine faces a geopolitical and security crisis which could lead to full-scale war. Here the need is twofold: First, to offer Ukraine military training, assistance, arms and equipment in order to defeat the separatist insurgents; Second, to deter the regime in Russia.

Deterring Russia, not only in Ukraine but elsewhere, is the hardest part of the task ahead. Russia is an integrated part of the world economy and of world decision-making on everything from space to subsea minerals. It cannot be simply isolated and ignored. But that does not mean that we cannot raise the cost of doing business for the Putin regime.

In particular, we should greatly extend the use of sanctions against individuals. The United States has commendably paved the way here with the Magnitsky Act—a move which other countries, sadly, have mostly so far failed to follow. The furious Russian reaction to the American imposition of even a handful of visa bans and asset freezes on those responsible for the death of the whistle-blowing auditor Sergei Magnitsky shows the effectiveness of this approach. The scope of such sanctions should be widened to include hundreds or even thousands of Russian decision-makers and policymakers. It could include all members of the legislature (Duma and Federation Council), all members of the General Staff, military intelligence (GRU) domestic security (FSB), foreign intelligence (SVR), the interior ministry (MVD) and other ''power agencies,'' the Presidential administration, and Presidential property administration (and companies which represent it abroad), companies run by personalities linked to the Putin regime, and any banks or other commercial institutions involved in doing business in occupied Crimea. Such visa bans and asset freezes could also be extended to the parents, children, and siblings of those involved.

This would send a direct and powerful message to the Russian elite that their own personal business in the West—where they and their families shop, study, save, and socialise—will not continue as usual. The United States should make vigorous overtures to its allies to encourage them to follow suit. The more countries which adopt sanctions, and the longer the list of those affected, the more pressure we are putting on the Putin regime to back off and change course.

We can also apply much tougher money-laundering laws to keep corrupt Russian officials out of the Western payments system and capital markets. We should intensify investigations of Russian energy companies which have mysterious origins, shareholders, or business models. We can tighten rules on trust and company formation agents to make it harder for corrupt Russian entities to exploit and abuse our system. It is often said that offshore financial centres are beloved by the Russian elite. But the shameful truth is that it is Britain and the United States which make life easiest for them.

We also need to improve the West's resilience and solidarity in the face of Russian pressure. American exports of LNG will be a small but welcome addition to the global natural gas market. Lithuania has built its own floating LNG terminal, which will become operational in December of this year, with the arrival of the aptly named ''Independence'' a vessel constructed in South Korea. Already, Gazprom's grip on Lithuania's natural gas market has slackened, and Lithuania has been able to negotiate a discount from the extortionate price—the highest in Europe—which the Russian gas giant had been charging. As energy editor of The Economist, I am sceptical of the idea that we will ever have a deep and liquid global LNG market: the technology and costs involved hinder the development of the needed supply chain. However at the margins, LNG does make a big difference, blunting the edge of any artificial emergency that Russia may try to create with selective supply interruptions.

Europe can do much more. It can build more gas storage, and liberalise the rules governing it, so that all parties have access to the facilities. It can complete the north-south gas grid, making it impossible for Russia to use supply interruptions on its four east-west export pipelines as a political weapon. Most of all, the European Commission should proceed with its complaint against Gazprom for systematic market-abuse and law-breaking. This move—in effect a prosecution—is based on the seizure of huge numbers of documents following raids on Gazprom offices and affiliates. The Commission had expected to release this complaint—in effect a charge sheet—in March. Then it was postponed until June. Many now wonder if it has been permanently shelved. The United States should urge the European Commission to enforce its laws.

I understand that the United States Justice Department is rightly suspicious of the way in which Russian companies operate in the world energy market. There are grave suspicions of price-fixing, insider trading, money-laundering and other abusive and illegal behaviour. My own researches suggest that these suspicions are amply justified, though writing about them is hampered by the costs and risks imposed by English libel law. In the course of researching the defence case in the libel case I mentioned earlier, I met several potential witnesses who were frightened for their physical safety if they cooperated with us. The more that the criminal justice system of the United States can do, through prosecution, witness protection and plea bargains, to drive the Russian gangster state out of international energy markets, the safer the world will be.

Next, we need to revive our information-warfare capability. We won the cold war partly because Soviet media lied as a matter of course, and ours did not. They tried to close off their societies from the free flow of information. We did not. In the end, their tactics backfired.

Just as we have underestimated the potential effect of Russian energy, money, and military firepower, so too have we neglected the information front. Russian propaganda channels such as the multilingual RT channel are well-financed and have made powerful inroads into our media space. They create a subtle and effective parallel narrative of world events, in which the West are the villains, mainstream thinking is inherently untrustworthy, and Russia is a victim of injustice and aggression, not its perpetrator.

Combating this will require a major effort of time, money, and willpower, involving existing media outlets, government, nonprofit organisations and campaigning groups. We need to play both defense and offense. We need to begin to rebut Russian myths, lies, and slanders, highlighting the factual inconsistences and elisions of the Kremlin narrative, and its dependence on fringe commentators and conspiracy theorists. We also need to start rebuilding the trust and attention we once enjoyed inside Russia. The collapse of respect and affection for the West inside Russia over the past 25 years has been a catastrophic strategic reverse, all but unnoticed in Western capitals. After the fall of communism, Russians believed we stood for freedom, justice, honesty, and prosperity. Now they believe that we are hypocritical, greedy, aggressive custodians of a failing economic system.

Finally, we need to reboot the Atlantic alliance. As memories fade of the Normandy beaches, of the Berlin Wall's rise and fall, and the sacrifice and loyalty of past generations, we are running on empty. Without a shared sense of economic, political, and cultural commonality, the Kremlin's games of divide and rule will succeed. This will require renewed and extraordinary efforts on both sides of the Atlantic. The revelations surrounding the secret material stolen by Edward Snowden have stoked fears in Europe that America is an unaccountable and intrusive global hegemon. This year I wrote a book—"The Snowden Operation" attacking the "Snowdenistas" as I termed the NSA renegade's unthinking defenders. I believe that our intelligence agencies as a rule function well, within the law, and to the great benefit of our nations. But much damage has been done. At a time when we need to be restoring transatlantic ties, they are withering before our eyes, especially in the vital strategic relationship with Germany. The Transatlantic Trade and Investment Partnership (TTIP) offers a rare chance of a big-picture, positive project which could help revive what sometimes looks like a failing marriage.

A final footnote: Whereas Russia once regarded the collapse of the Soviet Union as a liberation from communism, the regime there now pushes the line, with increasing success, that it was a humiliating geopolitical defeat. That is not only factually false; it is also a tragedy for the Russian people. They overthrew the Soviet Union, under which they had suffered more than anyone else. But they have had the fruits of victory snatched away by the kleptocratic ex-KGB regime. The bread and circuses it offers are little consolation for the prize that Russians have lost: a country governed by law, freed from the shadows of empire and totalitarianism, and at peace with itself and its neighbours.

Senator MURPHY. Ms. Shaffer.

40

STATEMENT OF BRENDA SHAFFER, PH.D., PROFESSOR, CENTER FOR RUSSIAN, EURASIAN AND EAST EUROPEAN STUDIES, GEORGETOWN UNIVERSITY, WASHINGTON, DC

Dr. SHAFFER. Chairman Murphy, Ranking Member Johnson, thank you for having this hearing this afternoon on this very important topic. The 21st century is the era of natural gas. In the 19th century coal was the dominant fuel, in the 20th century it was oil. But now enormous new natural gas resources have been discovered in vast new locations. Natural gas has many benefits, such as low environmental impact and lower carbon emissions than almost any other energy sources. Natural gas is the fuel that is most compatible with the use of renewable energy as a baseload in power generation.

However, security of supply in natural gas is more challenging than any other fuel source, as natural gas's physical qualities make it complicated and expensive to ship. Consequently, there is a greater need in the coming decades for meticulous policies and government involvement to ensure security of supply of natural gas.

A number of measures can improve European natural gas energy security. First, policy should focus on improving the security of supply in Europe's most vulnerable markets. Observers may speak of a single European energy market, but this is an illusion. States on Europe's periphery have much higher energy prices and bigger security challenges than those in the west and the center of Europe. The European Council's recently endorsed energy security strategy recognizes the uneven nature of this situation in Europe.

Natural gas sectors must be properly organized to guarantee security of supply regardless of the origin of the gas supplies or even the political situation. Supply disruptions most frequently result from technical glitches, natural disasters, or extreme weather. In fact, one of the biggest security challenges to natural gas supplies in recent years in Europe has been winter 2012 due to extreme weather.

Next, the United States and Europe should make sure that Kiev gets its natural gas sector in order. The Ukraine's unpaid gas bills to Gazprom are a legitimate Russian concern. Ukraine is the major transit point of Russian gas into Europe. In the last decade Ukrainian political elites across the political spectrum have engaged in reckless siphoning of gas, disregard for payments, and provided massive subsidies that encouraged runaway gas consumption. This behavior endangered security of supply to Europe.

Additional natural gas supplies can also improve the security of supply in Europe. The most promising new source of gas into Europe is the Southern Gas Corridor. Beginning in 2019, this project will bring natural gas from Azerbaijan into southern Europe. This project is the first in decades to bring new volumes into Europe and not just rerouting existing volumes.

This project also reaches the specific gas markets of southern Europe that have previously relied on a single source and are the most vulnerable. The Southern Gas Corridor can facilitate transport of increased volumes of gas from different sources, such as Iraq, such as the eastern Mediterranean, and any new sources that will be discovered in the region. Spurs can be built to additional markets in Europe, such as the Balkans. The project will bring thousands of new jobs in the construction phase to southern Europe, such as Albania, Greece, and Italy.

Azerbaijan made a strategic choice to sell its gas to Europe instead of to local markets that probably would have been more profitable, and Russia and Iran have noticed this strategic choice. This project needs continued EU and American support to make sure that Russia does not undermine it along the route. Russia may attempt to re-ignite the Nagorno-Karabakh conflict between Azerbaijan and Armenia or destabilize Georgia in order to thwart the development of the Southern Gas Corridor. Continued United States interest in resolving this conflict is important to removing the potential means for Russia to destabilize the region.

Another potential new source of natural gas into Europe is from Israel and Cyprus. The eastern Mediterranean at this point is too modest to serve as a source for mainland Europe unless additional discoveries are found. But this can be very useful for the region itself. The ability of these resources to serve as peace pipelines I believe are overstated. Energy trade reflects existing peaceful relations; it does not create them. In fact, dispute over energy resources or commercial conditions can exacerbate existing political conflicts and not resolve them, as we have seen so recently in Europe.

Although the gas volumes can eradicate conflicts in the Middle East over water as a source for desalination, essentially to remove any water shortages in the region. It has already increased water supplies to Israel, Jordan, and the Palestinian territories, at least removing this part of this quite regretful conflict. The new resources can also improve reliable and affordable electricity in this part of the Middle East, which is very important as a basis for future prosperity and hopefully for peace.

In recent months there has been some speculation that if a deal on Iran's nuclear program was reached with the West Teheran could also serve as a source of supply of gas to Europe. This idea is farfetched. While Iran indeed holds the second largest reserves of natural gas in the world, today Iran is, rather surprisingly, a net importer of natural gas, also fed by its huge domestic subsidies and inefficiency at home.

If Iran tried to launch a gas export project to Europe, Russia would surely block it. Over many issues, despite their semblance as allies, there is strategic competition between Iran and Russia, and especially in the sphere of natural gas exports.

Throughout Europe, Moscow employs sophisticated policies to continue its role as the dominant energy supplier in Europe and blocks indigenous production efforts in Europe and rival supply projects. For instance, Moscow sponsors and funds bogus environmental movements to oppose shale gas production and to oppose new gas projects. Professional government analysis should identify and disrupt these sophisticated organizations and companies that Moscow utilizes to protect its dominance in Europe and to remove the tax status, nonprofit status, for these organizations that receive this funding from Moscow. In addition, the EU should investigate Moscow's use of surrogate European and Russian companies that make nontransparent alliances with Russian companies and bar this behavior.

Another mechanism that Moscow can exploit is the manipulation of gas hub trade in Europe and this should be countered.

Last, Washington and Brussels should clarify to NATO and EU members that belong to these organizations that it entails also obligations to protect its energy security. Bulgaria's reluctance to implement policies intended to improve its own security of supply are particularly worrying.

Up until this year, Brussels has increasingly pulled out of the business of ensuring energy security and delegated the job to the invisible hand of the market. But the marketplace alone will not be enough to encounter a relentless Russia. National and EU institutions must take a more active and strategic role and the United States should support this.

Thank you.

[The prepared statement of Dr. Shaffer follows:]

PREPARED STATEMENT OF DR. BRENDA SHAFFER

The 21st century is the era of natural gas. In the 19th century, coal was the dominant fuel source and in the 20th century, it was oil. In the 21st century, enormous new natural gas sources have been discovered and produced. These new discoveries are vast in quantity and varied in location, with new parts of the globe becoming natural gas producers and new volumes far exceeding the rise in global demand for natural gas. Natural gas has many benefits as a fuel source, such as its low environmental impact and lower carbon emissions than most other energy sources. In many markets, it is also the cheapest source of energy for power generation and other functions. With these economic and environmental advantages, natural gas consumption has become widespread and in many places is supplanting coal as the main source of power generation. Natural gas is also the fuel that is most compatible with the use of renewable energy as a base load in power generation, and thus consumption of natural gas goes hand in hand with consuming of renewables under current technologies.

However security of supply is more challenging with natural gas than most other fuel sources, as natural gas' physical qualities make it complicated and expensive to ship. Consequently, there is a greater need in the coming decades for meticulous policies and government involvement to ensure security of supply of natural gas. The market alone will not create the infrastructure, multiple supply sources, storage, and contingency plans that can ensure security of supply.

In recent years, Europe has had a number of challenges in the sphere of energy security: carbon emissions are rising, high power generation costs are challenging the competitiveness of Europe's industry, and the security of the continent's natural gas supplies is tenuous. The recent Ukraine crisis serves as a new wake-up call regarding the importance of ensuring Europe's continued energy security.

The United States treats Europe's continued energy security as an integral part of U.S. national security policy. In recent years, the United States has significantly improved its capacity to integrate international energy policy into its foreign policy through the successful establishment of the State Department's Bureau of Energy Resources. In this recent crisis in Ukraine and in a number of arenas around the world, it is clear that this Bureau plays an important role in promoting U.S. national security and energy interests, including developing a comprehensive policy to improve European energy security in light of the recent crisis.

A number of measures can improve European natural gas energy security: focusing policies on specific markets in Europe that are at high risk for disruption of security of supply; respecting legitimate Russian commercial demands, such as payment for the gas it has shipped to Ukraine; developing new natural gas sources for Europe, especially the Southern Gas Corridor; identification organizations that are funded by Russia to undermine European energy security under the guise of promoting environmental protection; preventing European companies from acting as surrogates for Gazprom; halting potential price manipulation at gas sale hubs; requiring that NATO and EU members such as Bulgaria adopt EU energy security policies; and separating out EU climate change and renewable energy policies. In my testimony, I will elaborate on these policy suggestions and propose a policy approach for natural gas energy security policy in Europe.

A number of measures can improve European energy security:

- Focusing policies on specific markets in Europe that are at high risk for disruption of security of supply;
- Making payment to Russia for the gas it has shipped to Ukraine;
- Developing new natural gas sources for Europe, especially the Southern Gas Corridor;
- Identification of environmental movements that are funded by Russia to undermine European energy security;
- Preventing European companies from acting as surrogates for Gazprom;
- Halting potential price manipulation at gas sale hubs;
- Requiring that NATO and EU members such as Bulgaria adopt EU energy security policies;
- Separating EU climate change and renewable energy policies.

The natural gas supply situation in Europe is quite complex, and U.S. policies should focus on improving the security of supply in Europe's most vulnerable markets. Observers may speak of a single European energy market, but that is an illusion. States on Europe's periphery have much higher energy prices and bigger security challenges than those in the West and Center of Europe. The European Council's recently drafted Energy Security Strategy recognizes the uneven nature of the supply situation in Europe, and the EU is beginning to take positive steps to address this asymmetry.

Assessing a market's vulnerability to supply disruption depends on a number of factors, including the diversification of a state's fuel mix, its supply connections with neighbors, its capacity to switch to different fuels in power generation, the extent of its fuel storage (and especially natural gas storage) capacity, and the extent to which natural gas forms a part of a country's fuel mix.[1] Some markets, such as Germany, have multiple suppliers, and have energy infrastructure that connects it with neighbors. Other states, such as Poland, currently have access only to Russian natural gas, but natural gas is a small part of its power generation and total fuel consumption. Hungary also has only a single gas supplier, but it maintains extensive natural gas storage capacity and thus can easily endure supply disruptions.

Southern Europe and southeastern Europe contain some of the markets that are most vulnerable to potential natural gas supply disruptions. Not only do a number of the markets in the region rely on Russia as their single gas supplier, most of the markets in southern Europe are not interconnected by gas pipelines.

Natural gas sectors must be properly organized to guarantee security of supply, regardless of the origin of the supplies and the political situation. Supply disruptions most frequently result from technical glitches, natural disasters, or extreme weather. One of the biggest challenges in recent decades to the security of the natural gas supply in Europe took place in winter 2012 when severe cold weather created an extreme demand for gas, leaving some nations, such as Italy, Bulgaria, and Slovakia, without adequate supplies.

Price disruptions also hit European states in an uneven manner. States with multiple supply options, mostly in Western Europe, are able to contract gas for much lower prices than states located in Europe's periphery, such as in the continent's south and east, which rely mostly on supplies from Russia. Thus, natural gas energy security policies should target Europe's most vulnerable markets.

Next, the United States and Europe should make sure that Kiev gets its natural gas sector in order. In order to improve the security of energy supply, consumers should honor their contractual agreements with their Russian supplier. Ukraine's unpaid gas bills to Russian-led Gazprom, therefore, are a legitimate Russian concern. Ukraine is the major transit point for Russian gas into Europe. In the last decade, Ukrainian political elites across the political spectrum engaged in reckless siphoning of gas, disregarded payments, and provided massive subsidies that encouraged runaway gas consumption. In addition, Ukraine houses Gazprom's most important gas storage facilities. By acting as a reliable transit and storage partner, Kiev can create additional supply options for itself, from both neighbors in Europe and even Russia. However, companies will not utilize these immense storage facilities if they do not trust Ukraine to release these supplies or pay its bills.

Additional natural gas suppliers can also improve the security of supply in Europe. The most promising new source of gas into Europe is the Southern Gas Corridor. Beginning in 2019, this project will bring natural gas from Azerbaijan to southern Europe. This project is the first in decades to bring new volumes of natural gas into Europe (as opposed to only transiting existing supplies). This project also reaches specific gas markets of southern Europe that have previously relied primarily on a single source, leading to supply vulnerability and high import prices.

The Southern Corridor is a massive project, involving 7 countries, 6 regulatory systems, 12 investing companies, and costing $45 billion. It will bring significant investment and create tens of thousands of jobs in southern Europe. The Southern

Gas Corridor is an energy superhighway that can facilitate transport of increased volumes of gas from different sources, such as additional fields in Azerbaijan, Central Asia, Iraq, and potential production in the eastern Mediterranean. Spurs can be built from the Southern Corridor to reach additional markets in Europe, such as the Balkans. The project is being built with double the capacity that is needed for its current supply contracts and can be scaled up to a capacity of 60 BCM (2.2 tcf) annually in order to serve as a conduit for additional supplies into Europe. The Southern Gas Corridor will also serve as a catalyst for new interconnectors in Southern Europe and thus should help improve the supply situation in this region.

The Southern Corridor Natural Gas Pipeline

The State Department's Bureau of Energy Resources (and specifically Ambassador Carlos Pascual and Deputy Assistant Secretary Amos Hochstein) and Directorate-General for Energy of the European Commission, led by Commissioner Günther Oettinger, have played a vital role in cultivating this project and arriving at the final investment decision in December 2013. This project, however, needs continued support to ensure that Russia does not succeed in undermining it along the route. Final Investment Decision is only one stage in the process of establishing the Southern Gas Corridor.

Azerbaijan could have sold its natural gas at a higher profit to neighboring Iran and Russia, but embarked on the ambitious Southern Gas Corridor project in order to link itself with Europe and lower its dependence on these neighboring states. This strategic choice entails closer cooperation with Europe, Turkey, and the United States, but also elicits potentially negative responses from Russia and Iran, and thus needs U.S. and European political attention. Moscow may try to disrupt this project by supporting bogus environmental movements or using surrogate companies to buy infrastructure along the route. Russia may also attempt to reignite the Nagorno-Karabagh conflict between Azerbaijan and Armenia or destabilize Georgia in order to thwart the Southern Corridor. In May 2014, the U.S. representative to the OSCE Minsk Group, Ambassador James Warlick, made an important statement reaffirming the long-standing U.S. policy on the Nagorno-Karabakh conflict, and the State Department is attempting to invigorate the peace process between Azerbaijan and Armenia.[2] Continued U.S. interest in resolving the conflict is important for removing a potential means for Russia to destabilize the region.

Another potential new source of natural gas into Europe is from Israel and Cyprus. Eastern Mediterranean gas will only be able to serve as a source for mainland Europe if additional discoveries are found. At this point, there is most likely only 200 to 300 BCM (7–10.6 tcf) available for export, and these volumes would not justify a major new export project. Exploration is continuing and additional volumes may be discovered. Existing natural gas volumes, however, are still very useful in improving the energy security and prosperity for Cyprus, Israel, and their neighbors.

The discovery of significant reserves of offshore natural gas in Israel in 2009 and 2010 and rather smaller volumes of offshore natural gas in Cyprus in 2011 has sparked interest in their potential to contribute to regional cooperation and peace. These newfound resources, it is often said, can serve as peace catalysts and promote reconciliation between Israel and its neighbors, facilitate the reunification of Cyprus, and foster cooperation between Cyprus and Turkey. However, the probability that these new natural gas resources may serve as a lever for conflict resolution or produce far-reaching geopolitical effects is rather low. There is no evidence from elsewhere in the world that trading in energy is an incentive for peace. Case studies show no instances in which the incentive of energy trade led countries to make concessions on issues critical to peace agreements such as borders and the status of refugees.[3] Energy trade reflects existing peaceful relations; it does not create them. In many cases, the causal arrow points the other way; disputes over energy resources or commercial conditions of trade can exacerbate existing political conflicts.

While the new natural gas volumes may not serve as "peace pipelines," cooperation in the development of these resources can reinforce any political breakthroughs in the Middle East peace process or in efforts to find a comprehensive solution to the problem of the division of Cyprus. Moreover, the development of these resources has the potential to benefit the greater region by lowering the costs of desalination and increasing the supply of fresh water, and therefore these new natural gas reserves can contribute to the elimination of water conflicts in the region. The increased water supply enabled by the new natural gas volumes has already had a positive impact in the region. The new natural gas resources can also help the region by providing reliable and affordable electricity to the Palestinian territories, Jordan, and potentially to Lebanon and Syria. This is especially significant to a region where most countries' electricity supply is limited to certain hours of the day and where electricity production is unstable and cost-prohibitive.

In recent months, there has been some speculation that if a deal on Iran's nuclear program was reached with the West, Tehran could serve as a new supplier of natural gas to Europe and thus reduce dependency on Russia. This idea is quite far-fetched. While Iran indeed holds the second-largest natural gas volumes in the world, today Iran is, rather surprisingly, a net importer of natural gas. Due to low production volumes, huge domestic consumption, and low energy efficiency—all of which are exacerbated by gas price subsidies—Tehran imports today more gas than it exports (to Turkey and Armenia). In addition, if Iran tried to launch a gas export project to Europe, Russia would surely block it. In the past, Moscow has taken steps to block the entrance of Iran into European gas markets: in 2006, Gazprom bought a pipeline from Iran to Armenia and limited its size to ensure that it could be not be used to carry Iranian gas into Europe. While Russia and Iran may seem like allies, their cooperation is tacit. Over many issues there is strategic competition between Iran and Russia, and especially in the sphere of potential natural gas export.

As part of improving the security of supply, Europe must foil Moscow's effort to prevent new supplies from reaching Europe. Moscow employs sophisticated policies to continue its role as the dominant energy supplier in Europe and blocks indigenous production efforts in Europe and rival supply projects. For instance, Moscow sponsors and funds bogus environmental movements to oppose shale gas production in Europe and new gas pipeline projects. Astute, professional government analysis should identify and disrupt the sophisticated organizations and companies that Moscow utilizes to protect its dominance in Europe. Policies should be enacted that would remove the nonprofit status of these groups that collaborate with Russia and legislation similar to that that combats terror financing should bar European organizations from receiving funds from Moscow that are intended to promote Russia's foreign and security policy aims.

In addition, the EU should investigate Moscow's use of surrogate European and Russian companies and enact legislation that bars this behavior. Moscow attempts to gain influence over rival projects directly, via Russian companies, or indirectly, through closely allied companies in Europe, to hold on to its influence over the supply of gas to Europe. Gazprom and a number of European companies also use informal alliances to circumvent EU legislation meant to unbundle energy production, transmission, and distribution.

Another mechanism that Moscow can exploit to influence gas trade is manipulation of gas hub trade in Europe. The EU has encouraged the gas trade to transfer from long-term contracts with set prices or prices pegged to oil or other commodities to gas trade hubs with spot prices. Many new gas supply contracts signed in recent years have hub-based prices for part or all of their supplies. In Europe's case, the adoption of hub pricing may actually allow outside players to increase their hold on Europe. Gazprom, the largest source of gas traded currently on the continent's hubs, could manipulate hub prices by flooding or withholding gas from particular hubs to its own advantage. Policy mechanisms must be devised to prevent Russia or other actors from price manipulation at Europe's gas trade hubs.

The new EU energy security strategy calls for coordination among its members and solidarity after recognizing that the energy supply situation in eastern and southern Europe differs fundamentally from that of Western Europe. Eastern European states must embrace policies designed to boost their own long-term security and independence, and Washington and Brussels should clarify to NATO and EU members that belonging to these organizations entails obligations related to their energy infrastructure and security. Bulgaria's reluctance to implement policies in-

46

tended to improve its security of supply is particularly worrying, as it appears to reflect Russia's strong influence and frequent intervention in domestic political developments there.

Despite the EU's strong public support for policies to avert climate change, Europe's carbon emissions have risen in recent years. This is due primarily to the rise in coal consumption in Europe. It seems that Europe's failure to reduce its emissions emanates from the fact that it has linked its climate change policy to its renewable energy policies. Mandatory use of renewables has inadvertently encouraged utilities to use coal as a way to lower electricity production costs, thus contributing to the unintended consequence of rising emissions. In order to address this challenge, the EU needs to separate its climate change policy and renewable energy policy. Wind and solar power in their current technological states, regardless of how many subsidies are thrown at them, cannot deliver sufficient energy to current consumption demands. Europe needs climate change policies that address current consumption levels, with funds also invested in Europe's laboratories to discover the answers for the renewable future.

Ensuring Europe's natural gas security of supply entails a paradigm shift in energy policy. Up until this year, Europe's approach to the issue has focused on strengthening market mechanisms (''liberalization'') and reducing both EU and national government involvement in Europe's gas trade. Over the years, as the challenges have grown, Brussels has increasingly pulled European Union institutions and member states out of the business of ensuring energy security and delegated the job to the invisible hand of the market. But the marketplace alone will not be enough to counter a relentless Russia. National and EU institutions must take a more active, strategic role.

End Notes

[1] For more on natural gas supply disruptions and foreign policy, see Brenda Shaffer. ''Natural gas supply stability and foreign policy.'' Energy Policy 56 (2013): 114–125.
[2] http://www.state.gov/p/eur/rls/rm/2014/may/225707.htm.
[3] For more on ''peace pipelines,'' see Brenda Shaffer, ''Natural gas supply stability and foreign policy,'' Energy Policy 56 (2013), p. 6; Brenda Shaffer, Energy Politics (Philadelphia: University of Pennsylvania Press, 2009), pp. 70–74.

Senator MURPHY. Thank you.
Mr. Chow.

STATEMENT OF EDWARD C. CHOW, SENIOR FELLOW, ENERGY AND NATIONAL SECURITY PROGRAM, CENTER FOR STRATEGIC AND INTERNATIONAL STUDIES, WASHINGTON, DC

Mr. CHOW. Chairman Murphy, Ranking Member Johnson, I am honored to return to testify on European energy security and the impact of the ongoing crisis in Ukraine. When it comes to energy security for Europe, we focus primarily on natural gas supply. It is interesting to ponder why, when Europe is more dependent on oil imports than it is on gas imports. There has been major global oil supply interruptions in the past year, but not in gas. Yet the level of anxiety is much higher with gas than with oil. Why?

The root causes are in part related to incomplete market integration in Europe when it comes to gas and electricity. Its gas markets have been dominated until recently by long-term contracts at fixed volumes, with prices indexed to oil. Suppliers have restricted competition and the free flow of gas with destination clauses and control over pipelines.

These business practices were supported not only by major foreign suppliers, such as Gazprom, but also by incumbent European gas companies that control distribution networks in their home countries and pass on the higher cost of gas to consumers. Consequently, European markets in gas and electricity distribution infrastructure are not well connected for a supposed common market.

So what can the United States do to help our European allies and trading partners? The first point to be made is that we have already done a lot indirectly through the shale gas boom. Since the United States no longer imports liquefied natural gas in increasing volumes as expected, these supplies became available for Western Europe. Despite the initial denial of the lasting nature of the shale gas phenomenon, Gazprom was forced to meet the market by adjusting downward all its major supply contracts under more flexible pricing terms. As a result, European imports of Russian gas increased by 13 percent last year, half of which transits through Ukraine.

Western European LNG import facilities are currently operating at very low utilization rates. Even if U.S. LNG exports were available today, they would not be imported by Europe, but by East Asia, where spot gas prices are about double European prices.

When the United States begins to export major volumes of LNG in a few years, its benefits to Europe lies not in the quantities it might receive, but in future price formulation in global gas markets. International gas prices may no longer rise and fall with oil prices, with prices in different regions converging as a result of U.S. exports.

The competitive advantage the shale gas revolution provided the U.S. economy, with lower gas and electricity prices coupled with reduced greenhouse gas emissions, has also caused Europeans to reexamine their energy policies, with renewed efforts for further market liberalization, enforcement of competition rules, and rethink on the use of domestic energy resources.

In the mean time, the crisis in the Ukraine caused by Russian action presents a clear and present danger for European energy security. The risks are borne disproportionately by Central and Eastern European countries since they rely on Russia for almost all their gas imports, much of which transits through Ukraine. Ukraine's weak and corrupt energy sector creates severe vulnerabilities for itself and its neighbors.

The previous Ukrainian Government left the current government with mounting gas debt to Russia. This debt and the failure to agree to new gas prices led to the cutoff of Russian supplies to Ukraine on June 16. Ukraine depends on Russia normally for 60 percent of its gas demand and is the major transit corridor for Russian gas exports through Europe. In neither case are there ready substitutes.

If the already-delayed injection of gas into strategically located western Ukrainian storage facilities does not begin soon, Ukraine will run out of gas before the start of winter. If nothing changes, the Ukrainian Government would be left this winter with a choice of either letting its own population freeze or taking gas from Russia destined for European markets for its own use.

If Russia's intent is to further destabilize Ukraine and to prove to Europe that Ukraine is an unreliable transit partner, then it is in Russia's interest to prolong negotiations. To date, European mediation has not led to any real results. The European gas market is surprisingly complacent about the situation. Spot gas prices have dropped significantly. Although gas storage capacity has risen, actual storage is not as high as it could be. The risk of miscalculation is high.

Meanwhile, Russia is pushing its South Stream gas pipeline, which would bypass Ukraine altogether, as an alternative supply route to Europe.

As someone more comfortable with commercial negotiations, I instinctively question economic negotiations brokered by political leaders. I will know the EU-mediated Russian-Ukrainian gas negotiations have become serious when negotiators stop talking to the press.

Long-term sustainable economic transactions cannot be based mainly on political conditions, which tend to change, as we discovered with the Russian-Ukrainian gas deals of January 2006, January 2009, April 2010, and last November. Raising matters to the highest political level, as Europe has done, only invites Russia to make political demands, such as accommodation of its occupation of Crimea, restrictions on Kiev's actions in southeastern Ukraine, and stopping further Western economic sanctions resulting from Russian aggression against Ukraine.

The only real solution to the crisis in Ukraine is to strengthen Ukraine. President Poroshenko, Prime Minister Yatsenyuk, Energy Minister Prodan all observed firsthand and up close the blunders made by previous Ukrainian Governments on energy policy. Business as usual is no longer an option. Concrete policy action is required and we have seen precious little so far.

What needs to be done for energy sector reform in Ukraine is well known, especially in natural gas. What have been missing are the political will and the professional and financial capacity to execute reforms in an orderly and systematic way.

Reform depends foremost on Ukrainian leaders. True reformers deserve and require concerted Western assistance if they are to be successful. As long as Ukraine is weak, it is an open invitation for Russian opportunism and aggression and a constant source of instability in the heart of Europe.

Neither Ukraine nor the West will have another chance better than the opportunity created by the current crisis for energy reform. The situation cries out for American leadership, working closely with Europe and the donor community, by injecting needed resources with strict conditionality on the provision of assistance. Our policy must be informed by sound analysis, not wishful thinking, followed by hard work.

Thank you.

[The prepared statement of Mr. Chow follows:]

PREPARED STATEMENT EDWARD C. CHOW

Chairman Murphy, Ranking Members Johnson, members of the committee, it is an honor for me to return to the subcommittee to testify on European energy security and the impact of the ongoing crisis in Ukraine.

When it comes to the question of energy security for Europe, we are, of course, talking primarily about natural gas supply. It is interesting to ponder why, when Europe is more dependent on oil imports than it is on gas imports. In the past year, there were major oil supply interruptions from unrest in Libya, sanctions against Iran, and minor disruptions from Syria and South Sudan. On the other hand, there has been no gas supply cutoff to Europe even with the Ukraine crisis caused by Russia's actions. Russia's share of the European oil market is about the same as it is with gas. Yet the level of anxiety in Europe is much higher with gas than with oil. Why?

The answers go beyond the different nature of oil and gas markets and the ease that crude oil and petroleum products can be traded and transported as compared to natural gas. The root causes are related to incomplete market integration in Europe when it comes to gas and electricity, which fails to take full advantage of economies of scale provided by a 500-million consumer market.

Europe has not adapted to changes in the global gas market or adapted to new technologies. Its gas markets have been dominated until recently by long-term contracts at fixed volumes with prices indexed to oil. Suppliers have restricted competition and the free flow of gas with destination clauses and control of pipelines. Consequently, Europe does not enjoy gas-on-gas competition the way we do in the United States after the Federal Government deregulated natural gas in 1978, which incidentally was a major factor enabling our shale gas revolution.

Many of these anticompetitive business practices were supported not only by major foreign suppliers such as Gazprom of Russia, but also by incumbent European gas companies that control distribution infrastructure in their home countries and were all too happy to pass on the higher cost and economic pain of an inflexible system to gas consumers. Consequently, European gas and electricity distribution infrastructure and markets are not as well connected as one might suppose in a common market.

So what can the United States do to help our European allies and trading partners? Here I have to debunk some commonly held notions in Washington.

The first point that has to be made is we have already done a lot indirectly through the shale gas boom. Since the United States no longer imports liquefied natural gas (LNG) in increasing volumes as we were expected to do, these supplies from liquefaction projects previous targeted for the U.S. market became available for Western Europe. Despite initial denial of the lasting nature of the shale gas phenomenon, Gazprom was forced to meet the market by adjusting downward all its major supply contracts under more flexible pricing. As a result, European imports of Russian gas increased by 13 percent last year, half of which transits through Ukraine. Western European LNG import facilities are currently operating at very low utilization rates (around 25 percent). Even if U.S. LNG exports were available today, they would not be imported by Western Europe, but by East Asia where spot gas prices are about double European prices.

When the United States begins to export major volumes of LNG in a few years, its benefit to Europe lies not in the quantities it might receive, but in future price formulation in global gas markets. We may finally see gas-on-gas competition outside of North America, with gas prices no longer rising and falling with oil prices, when global market prices converge after adjusting for LNG transportation cost differential.

The tremendous competitive advantage the shale gas revolution has provided the U.S. economy, with lower gas and electricity prices coupled with reduced greenhouse gas emissions, has also caused European capitals and the European Union (EU) to reexamine their energy policies, with renewed efforts for further market liberalization, enforcement of competition rules, and rethink on the use of domestic energy sources. (It is not without irony that some advocate strongly for exporting U.S. LNG to our European allies when some of these countries, such as France and Germany, effectively ban hydraulic fracturing.) However, it will take years before significant results can be achieved.

In the meantime, the crisis in Ukraine, caused by Russia, presents a clear and present danger for European energy security. The risks are borne disproportionately by Central and Eastern European countries, as I testified before this subcommittee in April, since they rely on Russia for almost all of their gas imports, much of which transits through Ukraine. I also testified before this subcommittee 2 years ago on the vulnerability Ukraine's weak and corrupt energy sector creates for itself and its neighbors. I wish I could be more optimistic today than I was in those two other occasions.

The previous Ukrainian Government left the current government with mounting gas debt to Russia, which predates President Yanukovych's public change of heart on the signing of the Association Agreement with Europe last November. The debt issue and the failure to agree to new gas prices led to the cutoff of Russian gas supply to Ukraine on June 16. Ukraine depends on Russia normally for 60 percent of its gas supply and is the major transit corridor for Russian gas exports to Europe. In neither case are there ready substitutes.

If the already delayed injection of gas into strategically located western Ukrainian storage facilities does not begin soon, Ukraine will run out of gas before the start of winter. If nothing changes, the Ukrainian Government would be left with a choice of either letting its own population freeze or taking gas from Russia destined for European markets for its own use.

If one assumes that Russia's intent, unless met with stiff resistance, is to further destabilize Ukraine and to prove to Europe that Ukraine is an unreliable transit partner, then it is in Russia's interest to prolong current negotiations. To date, European mediation has led to no results other than agreement on the date and place for the next round of negotiations. The European gas market is surprisingly complacent about the situation. Spot gas prices have dropped significantly and, although gas storage capacity has risen, actual storage is not as high as it could be. The risk of miscalculation is high.

Meanwhile Russia is pushing its South Stream gas pipeline project, which would bypass Ukraine altogether, as an alternative supply route to Europe. Only yesterday Russian Foreign Minister Lavrov was in Sofia urging Bulgaria to start construction of its segment of South Stream against EU objection. (Incidentally Bulgaria also bans shale gas exploration.) Long ago Russia has signed up the west Balkan countries along the route to support South Stream; more recently Austria came onboard formally. Gazprom's partners in South Stream include major Italian, German and French energy companies. Partners such as the Western-supported Southern Gas Corridor projects of Trans-Anatolian pipeline (TANAP) and Trans-Adriatic pipeline (TAP) have not progressed as fast as was hoped after contract signings at the end of last year. For example, the landing spot in Italy has not yet been agreed.

As someone more comfortable with commercial negotiations, I instinctively question economic negotiations brokered by political leaders eager to head to the press conference after a couple of hours of unproductive discussions. I will know the negotiation has become serious when negotiators stop talking to the press. Some of the proposals on gas from European politicians, such as an energy union with a single gas purchaser (Polish Prime Minister Tusk) and a uniform gas price for Europe (EU Energy Commissioner Oettinger) make no economic or commercial sense and are, I hope, merely political posturing and not serious policy proposals.

Long-term sustainable economic transactions cannot be based mainly on political conditions, which tend to change as we discovered with the Russia-Ukraine gas deals of January 2006, January 2009, April 2010, and last November. Raising matters to the highest political level as Europe has done only invites Russia to make political demands, such as accommodation of its occupation of Crimea, restrictions on Kiev's actions in southeastern Ukraine, and a stop to further Western economic sanctions in response to Russian aggression against Ukraine. These negotiations need to be handled in a professional manner yet to be displayed by any side.

The only real solution to the crisis in Ukraine is to strengthen Ukraine itself. It has been more than 4 months since the acting Ukrainian Government came into power after the collapse of the previous government. President Poroshenko was inaugurated almost exactly a month ago. He, Prime Minister Yatsenyuk, Energy Minister Prodan all observed firsthand and up close the blunders made by previous Ukrainian governments on energy policy by perpetuating and expanding the corrupt system. Business-as-usual is no longer an option and cannot be accepted, especially by the Ukrainian people after the sacrifices of EuroMaidan which they continue to make. Policy rhetoric alone is insufficient. Concrete action is required and we have seen precious little so far. Some initial steps, such as the emergency energy legislation proposed by the government and passed by the Ukrainian Parliament (Rada) in its first reading last Friday, appear to be against market principles and require more professional scrutiny.

What needs to be done for energy sector reform in Ukraine is well known, especially in natural gas. Many studies have been commissioned in the past decade by Ukrainian governments and international bodies, and have gathered dust. What have been missing are the political will and the professional and financial capacity to execute reforms in an orderly and systematic way. This is particularly important in pricing reform not only at the consumer level as demanded by the International Monetary Fund (IMF), but also at the producer level in order to encourage investments in domestic production. Also crucial are a truly independent energy regulatory commission and transparent, modern licensing procedures to eliminate graft.

Reform depends foremost on Ukrainian leaders. True reformers deserve and require concerted Western assistance if they are to succeed. More than 20 years of neglect has left Ukraine with meager financial and human resources to fundamentally reform its energy sector, which is so critical to its survival and to stability in the region. As long as Ukraine is weak, it is an open invitation for Russian opportunism and aggression, and a constant source of instability in the heart of Europe.

The West took its eye off the ball after the Orange Revolution in 2004 and never gave President Yushchenko and his various cabinets the tough love they needed. After 2010, we appeared to avert our eyes capriciously with President Yanukovych and his barely disguised industrial-strength corruption. Neither Ukraine nor the West will have another chance better than the opportunity created by the current crisis. The situation cries out for American leadership, working closely with Europe and the donor-community, by injecting needed resources with strict conditionality on the provision of assistance. Similar to Ukraine, our own rhetoric must also be informed by sound analysis and followed by concrete actions, not wishful thinking as we have done too many times with Ukraine and its energy sector in the past.

Senator MURPHY. Thank you very much. Thank you, all of you, for your testimony.

Mr. Chow, I wanted just to ask you a question about the effect of a prolonged crisis in Ukraine. You posit that it would accrue to Russia's benefit because it would undermine faith in Ukraine on behalf of the EU. I think there are sort of three, in my mind, three possible outcomes, and I am sure you can add to them.

One is the one that you suggest, that it will undermine European faith in Ukraine and compromise, enthusiasm for marrying together Ukraine and the EU or ultimately with NATO. Second, it could increase enthusiasm for alternate routes of gas to Europe. South Stream is the primary example. But it could also be a tremendous wake-up call, the straw that breaks the camel's back, in terms of prompting Europe to do the things truly necessary to become much more energy-independent of Russia.

Why is the third—why is my third alternative not just as plausible as the first two?

Mr. CHOW. Thank you, Senator, for that important question. I hope you are right, but I think if you were sitting in Russia's shoes: Europe got a wake-up call in January 2006 when gas was cut off to Ukraine. It got another wake-up call in January 2009, when, instead of a three-day gas cutoff, Europe suffered a 3-week gas cutoff. It has done precious little so far except for the steps that I have already mentioned. Its response to the invasion of Crimea, as well as Russia's adventurism, may I say, in southeastern Ukraine has been relatively weak and disunited.

So I think from—I guess it is a parlor game now to try to get into Vladimir Putin's head. But from his standpoint, the way he sees it—and he may be miscalculating—the time is on his side, not on Europe or Ukraine's side.

Senator MURPHY. Let me ask that question of the other three panelists. A simple question—it is not simple: Does a prolonged crisis harm Ukraine more, or Russia more, with respect to future dynamics over EU membership or future continued reliance on European energy? Mr. Lucas, you have your hand up, so I will go to you and then Ms. Shaffer and then Mr. Simonyi.

Mr. LUCAS. I think Europe frequently gets wake-up calls and it then goes back to sleep again. I think that the question here is the timeframe. I slightly disagree with Mr. Chow, that I think that the previous crises have stimulated quite a lot of activity in Europe. We do now have a pretty much complete north-south gas grid. We have quite better storage. We have the Third Energy Package, which has reduced Russia's monopoly power.

This means that if they cut the gas off right now we would have about 3 months before it would start to bite, and that is quite nice. But in terms of the sort of stuff you were talking about to make a real difference, we are talking years. If we start right now, in 5 years time we would have a really resilient energy system. If not a fully independent one, but at least a Europe that had lots of LNG capacity, lots of storage, new interconnectors to Norway, all this sort of stuff. But the gap between 3 months and 5 years is the vulnerability.

What Russia knows is that they can threaten stuff, which scares politicians. Just like here, we have a fragile recovery and the politicians are desperate not to have stuff that is going to harm growth and jobs and so on. An energy interruption, or worries about energy and what that does to business confidence, is a powerful weapon for the Russians. They just have to threaten this stuff and we already start thinking of ways of trying to make this conflict go away, rather than try to win it.

Senator MURPHY. Ms. Shaffer.

Dr. SHAFFER. I think with the last move of Russia they set up a really perfect strategy. They actually set up Ukraine against Europe, because basically the gas is still flowing to Europe and the only way for Ukraine to get the gas is actually to disrupt the supplies to Europe and not put gas into storage to meet future commitments. So actually in the long run, as winter approaches it is pinning Kiev against Europe.

I would say that if you look at previous European response to these crises, it was actually to build North Stream, meaning building a pipeline directly from Russia to Germany that circumvents transit states. Again, as you said, you might see the response being South Stream, or the more responsible response would be the Southern Corridor.

While the Third Energy Package is great in terms of principles and in a very perfect world where lawyers run all the gas trade, it is very nice. But I think in the reality of Russian behavior, as we pointed out, whether it is manipulation of gas hubs, of price— Gazprom is the biggest trader in Europe's gas hubs, so of course they can flood the market, deny the market, and really affect these prices.

I think what we need in Europe is a paradigm change. They based the Third Energy Package on the American model, which is—what you have, the market has done a great job here in increasing U.S. energy security. But the United States has been able to succeed due to the unique structure of its market. The United States has thousands of gas buyers, hundreds of gas producers. The largest gas producer in the United States only has 3 percent of the market. Europe has three gas producers. Three of them, all three, are external to Europe and each has about a third of the market. It is a completely different game.

What Europe needs is a paradigm shift. Gas is not a commodity. Gas is a utility. When we grew up we called gas a utility, not something that you just trade. When you think of it as a utility, it is a public good, which needs much more public involvement.

Senator MURPHY. Ambassador.

Mr. SIMONYI. I think what really is at stake is a competition of two systems, our liberal societies and Putin's ideas; he is going to use the time before we get our acts together to export his illiberal ways of running a society.

The signs that you encountered in Bulgaria are exactly this. He is targeting the weakest links within Europe and within the NATO alliance. Also one of the really big problems is not directly related to energy, but that the perception of the Russian threat is very, very different in Western Europe, northern Europe, southern Europe, and Eastern Europe. In Eastern Europe I am really worried, that Russia with multiple tools in its toolbox, expecially Putin using energy, and other kinds of tools, can easily influence particularly the Eastern and Central European countries. Putin feels this was once part of his sphere of influence and it is just unfair that they are now on the other side.

Senator MURPHY. I will save my other questions for the second round.

Senator Johnson.

Senator JOHNSON. Mr. Ambassador, you asked for a softball, so I will throw it to you. What is Putin thinking?

Mr. SIMONYI. I think what Putin is thinking right now is, first of all: My goal was to destabilize Ukraine enough so that it is definite that the Ukraine will not be part of the Western institutions, the European Union or NATO. This was his first goal. I think he has achieved that, and he is going to resort to all kinds of means to stoke trouble when the moment comes and it looks like things are too smooth.

I think for now he is totally satisfied with running or ''owning,'' the Crimea, and I have no doubt that, at any moment he can turn the switch on and we will be back to a lot of trouble. The fact that we do not see him visibly present in the eastern Ukrainian conflict at this moment does not mean that he is not fully in control of the insurgencies.

Senator JOHNSON. Mr. Lucas.

Mr. LUCAS. I think Mr. Putin thinks that we are weak and he is winning.

Senator JOHNSON. I agree.

I was always in support of strong sanctions, hopefully targeted ones that were really painful to Putin, not to us. When we were talking of all these sanctions, that they were a double-edged sword, I really wanted to stop talking about them because I thought it was just a delaying action, they were not going to be implemented, and they had no effect.

When we were in Poland—I do not want to identify the individual telling us this, but I think we have had this since confirmed—apparently 100 to 110 Russians control 35 percent of the wealth. Certainly being from the outside, hearing how effective the sanctions were against North Koreans, just the top leaders, denying them their access to their banking accounts and traveling to Macau and that type of thing, was the most effective sanction, why do we not target in a far more robust fashion those 100 to 110 individuals in Russia that really do rely on the West for their banking, for their wealth dispersion, that type of thing? Mr. Lucas, I will go to you.

Mr. LUCAS. Well, I could not agree with you more, Senator. I think that we are looking for kind of magic sanctions that do not hurt us and do hurt Putin. Unfortunately, there are no such things. Every country has got something to lose, because Russia has done a very good job of building up vulnerabilities and dependencies.

But I do think these visa sanctions and asset freezes are a really powerful weapon. We have not begun to exploit them. We have laws against money-laundering in my country and in your country. Banks are supposed to know their customer before they start taking deposits. So how is it possible these people on their modest official salaries and their sons and daughters and wives and parents and all the rest of it are coming and putting tens and hundreds of millions of dollars through our payments system and through our financial system?

How is it possible that Rosneft was allowed to list on the London Stock Exchange, when Rosneft feasted on the corpse of Yukos? You remember, Russia's biggest oil company was dismembered because of a political fight with the Kremlin. Rosneft buys its assets for nothing, $8 billion of Western shareholders' money goes down the tube, and then this company, which is effectively taking stolen property, is allowed to list on one of the oldest, most reputable stock exchanges. How is that possible?

The old Russian dissidents had a great slogan, which was: "Powers that be, enforce your laws." "Vlast soblyudaite zakoniy!" I think we should just start enforcing our own laws, and we would be amazed at the scope.

On visas, we do not have to just start with these people. The most terrifying thing in Russia is not the secret police; it is an angry Russian woman. If these people are going home at night and finding that their wives and grandmothers and daughters are all saying, we cannot study in the West any more, we cannot shop in the West any more, we cannot go on vacation in the West any more, because of these visa sanctions applying to us, that would really hurt.

Senator JOHNSON. Does it not also threaten the oligarchs when they cannot spread their money around the world? I would not want to be an oligarch in Russia, fall out of favor with Putin, and have all my wealth in Russia.

Mr. LUCAS. The first thing they do is they get foreign passports. They get Finnish citizenship and Swiss citizenship. They move their assets offshore. They diversify, because they realize what a mess Russia is in. We have a wonderful opportunity there to hurt them.

Senator JOHNSON. Mr. Ambassador, do you want to chime in?

Mr. SIMONYI. Yes. We know there is much more grumbling in the inner circles of Putin about the sanctions than meets the eye.

Senator JOHNSON. So let me ask: Why do we not do it?

Mr. SIMONYI. That I do not know. I think Putin thinks that he can count on the divide between America and Europe——

Senator JOHNSON. Again, we are showing more weakness, playing right into his hands.

Mr. SIMONYI. I think so.

Senator JOHNSON. Mr. Lucas, what is the EU thinking by not dropping those charges on Gazprom, not revealing to the public what they found in their investigations? What is the EU thinking? Because what would be a more perfect, totally directed sanctions to a certain extent, when Putin is invading Crimea and threatening peace in the Ukraine? What could be more effective than that? What are they thinking?

Mr. Lucas. I think in a way it was too perfect, that it was seen as an enormous escalation of a response, when the conventional wisdom, which I believe is wrong in both this country and in Europe, was we need to find an exit ramp for Putin, we do not want to escalate this, we are not going to send massive naval task forces to the Black Sea, we are trying to apply very judicious, moderate sanctions, raise the cost for Putin, and give him a chance to back down, and launching this equivalent of a kind of cruise missile straight at the Kremlin was not seen as part of that.

I think that was wrong. I think that postponing it makes him think the Russians will always hope that there will be a political solution to this. They have said again and again to the European Union: Do not go down this quasi-prosecutorial, quasi-judicial route; let us have a political deal; we will agree to stop doing some stuff and maybe pay a little bit of fines here and there, but we do not want a big public fight.

I fear that that argument has begun to bite, and I think it is a great pity. It would have been a wonderful thing to see this prosecution of Gazprom, and I am beginning to wonder if we are ever going to see it. Certainly it was hoped that it was going to be under this Commission, but it looks to me at the moment as though it is going to be passed to the next Commission. And we do not, of course, know what the political complexion and makeup of that Commission will be.

Senator Johnson. Thank you all. I will complete mine in the next round.

Senator Murphy. Mr. Lucas, you said twice that you think Russia is winning, so I want to pursue that rather simplistic rendering of geopolitics. I guess if the measurement is levels of testosterone and bravado, he is winning. If the measurement is the respective approval ratings of Putin versus Obama, he is winning. But when I look at other metrics, it is hard for me to understand how he is winning. He has less friends now than he had before. Former republics are climbing over themselves to sign association agreements with the European Union and are only stopped by illegal tactics and invasions.

His economy is in recession, two straight quarters likely of negative growth, massive capital flight, U.S. banks that will not do any business with them. He is no longer a member of the G8. He is not an international pariah, but he certainly has less influence than he used to.

We are having a debate here about how fast Europe is going to move away from Russian energy, but I do not think there is any debate as to whether the next 10 years will see more or less reliance. It is just at what pace.

So how is he winning if he has less friends, his economy is in worse shape, he has been kicked out of international institutions, and his reason for existence, being an energy supplier to Europe, is in peril?

Mr. Lucas. I think that is a bit like saying to—first of all, I completely agree with you. But it is a bit like saying to Tony Soprano: Doesn't it bother you that you don't have any friends? And he says: I have lots of money and the people who need to be scared of me are scared of me.

So in his terms—and the question was what is going on inside his head—he thinks this is great. A few years ago, a couple of years ago, Putin was in trouble in Russia because basically the Putin modernization program has not worked, Russia has not diversified, the infrastructure is still rubbish, public services are still rubbish. And he was becoming a bit of a figure of ridicule and the opposition was doing quite well. That has all changed now. The opposition is nowhere, ratings are high, and he has kind of distracted Russian public opinion through these foreign adventures.

Yes, you are absolutely right that countries like Kazakhstan are very nervous, Moldova, Georgia, and so on. Even Belarus is kind of wobbling. But he does not care about that. When he needs them to do something, he can make them do it. And he sees that he has got more influence now in Western Europe or in Europe than he had ever dreamed of. The Atlantic alliance is weak.

The success of this divide and rule strategy has been pretty impressive. You only have to look at the way countries are signing up for South Stream, the enormous wave of anti-Americanism we are seeing in Germany right now with the Snowden stuff. There is a whole range of things that must make him think the sun is shining.

Senator MURPHY. Ambassador.

Mr. SIMONYI. I wanted to add to this that he does not necessarily want to be seen winning; he wants to win, meaning that while we are debating Ukraine, while we are debating energy, at the same time he is doing a lot of other things in Europe. He is buying up banks, he is buying up companies. What he wants is a long-term influence within the European Union and within NATO. So in that sense, I think in a way he is winning. He is not winning in the sense that we consider winning, but he is winning in the sense, in his own world, he is going to gain a foothold that will be very difficult to counter if we are not very careful.

Senator MURPHY. I just think that is an enormously important distinction, because I do not really care if he thinks that he is winning according to his terms. We have to conduct our business according to our understanding of winning, losing, what benefits us, what is to the detriment of U.S. security interests.

Let me turn the topic to another, more specific issue. That is this intersection of production and transmission. When we were in Romania there was some very positive discussion about the ability to move Romanian resources into Moldova, save for the fact that the Russians owned a controlling stake in the transmission lines inside Moldova. So all the work that was going to go into moving the product to the border of Moldova was potentially for naught, because once you got it into the country it was still up to Russia.

The Third Energy Package speaks to this in trying to separate the two. But how important is this control of transmission to Russian energy hegemony and what are the prospects to dislodge their control of transmission? Is there anything that the United States can do about that? I am asking that to the panel. So, Ms. Shaffer, you seem most eager to answer.

Dr. SHAFFER. This is a crucial—Senator Murphy, thank you for this question because it is crucial. In a sense, the Third Energy Package has created opportunity for Russia to actually get its hands on transmission systems, because the producers or other shippers or distributors cannot own it. So these things have gone for sale. Also, with the financial crisis in a number of countries in the region, there has been privatization of transmission systems. So this has given them incredible leverage within Europe.

So for instance, as the Southern Corridor made a decision to go through Southern Europe and go on the route of Greece, Albania, and Italy, suddenly we see a small Russian unknown company pop up and suddenly try to buy the transmission system, DESFA, in Greece. They are quite aware that this is a way that, if you cannot beat them with a South Stream at least try to buy a chunk from within.

So something has to be done, because the Third Energy Package actually will enable this kind of behavior and not the opposite. We see, for instance, exactly as you pointed out in the case of Moldova, that Russia is constantly taking payment for gas in national infrastructure. In January, Armenia lost its last stake in its gas transmission infrastructure. It became Gazprom Armenia. In the end, this might even be more hurting of a state's independence than actually its gas supplies, because this becomes an actor in the local economy and gives it a lot of leverage as one of the major financial forces domestically in the country.

Senator MURPHY. Mr. Chow, your thoughts on this question?

Mr. CHOW. I would support what Dr. Shaffer said. The idea of piling up debt in order to have a debt-equity swap later is a long-standing Russian business model since the collapse of the Soviet Union. It happened inside Russia and it applies in Moldova's case as well. The reason Gazprom is controlling equity is for all the gas debt that Moldova owes Gazprom, including, by the way, gas that was actually utilized by Transnistria and not paid for. So this is quite a common practice by Russia.

The EU leverage that on paper could be applied is the fact that these countries, including Moldova and Ukraine, by the way, are signatories to the European Energy Community Treaty and are supposed to comply over time with the acquis communautaire energy of the European Union. That has been observed mainly in the breach in the case of both Ukraine and Moldova up until now. But this is certainly something within the EU's power to police over time. It has chosen not to do so for reasons that my European colleagues may know more than I do.

Senator MURPHY. Senator Johnson.

Senator JOHNSON. I want to go back to the issue of winning, because I think it is just a crucial point. If we do not understand what the objective of our adversaries is, we will misjudge. So I do not believe Putin is acting rationally from the standpoint of improving his economy. I agree with you, Mr. Chairman. This is not long-term in Russia's best interest, but it is in the best interest of Vladimir Putin. I think this is all about Vladimir Putin, about his ego, about his power, about his control.

Mr. Lucas, in your testimony you were talking about when we expanded NATO, we did not even draw up contingency plans for the military defense of the new members because we assumed Russia was a friend. Now, we all hoped that. I wish at this point Russia was a friendly rival. But they are not a friendly rival. They are an adversary. I am hoping they do not become a full-fledged enemy.

Mr. Lucas, I want to ask you again: What do you think is Vladimir Putin's goal personally? What is he in this for?

Mr. LUCAS. I think, first of all, lots of money, to be honest. Secondly, I think he wants to weaken the West to the point that he does not think we are a threat to him. So he wants to corrupt, corrode, and coerce Europe, and he is doing a pretty good job of it.

I think he worries that successful countries on his borders might give his people ideas. We, I think quite wrongly, in the European Union thought that Russia would be happy if we could make Ukraine into a success story. We thought it would be nice for Russia to have a large, successful, prosperous, well-governed, law-abiding neighbor with a free press and contested elections and so on, and this would be a great thing for Russia.

I tried again and again to explain to European Union officials that if we try to make a success of Ukraine that is an existential threat to Putin and he will react very strongly. And they said: We do not believe in geopolitics. And I said: You may not believe in geopolitics, but geopolitics believes in you.

Senator JOHNSON. But explain a little bit further why that is an existential threat to Putin. If Putin has got successful democracies that are Western-leaning, lacking corruption, or have reduced corruption, and his citizens are seeing that in Ukraine, is that the reason it is an existential threat?

Mr. LUCAS. Yes. For example, Ukraine would be the second-largest Russian media space in the world, and if you have tens of millions of people consuming Russian media and fostering a lively culture of debate and inquiry, some of those debates and inquiries will start touching on Russia, and Russians will start watching that. He needs to be able to tell Russians that: My way is the only way and nothing else works.

Senator JOHNSON. So successful bordering countries threaten his power, threaten his control. This is true. When I first made my trip to the region in 2011 we went up to the border in Georgia, where they had invaded. They were all talking about how Vladimir Putin at that point in time was doing everything he possibly could to undermine their success, undermine their democracies.

Mr. LUCAS. I think you have put your finger on a very important point, which is that these front-line states have been warning us in the West about this even before Putin.

Senator JOHNSON. And we just refuse to acknowledge it because it does not make sense to us. Why would anybody do that? We all wanted integrated economies, we want to lift up everybody's lifestyle. That is not what Putin is trying to do.

Mr. LUCAS. Absolutely, we patronized them, we belittled them, we ignored them, we told them they had their hair on fire. And they have been proved right. I think the first thing we should do is that we should ask them for advice. We should say: What do you think we should be doing? You actually know this problem better than we do. What is your suggestion?

Senator JOHNSON. What a concept, go to the real experts.

Mr. Ambassador.

Mr. SIMONYI. I agree, we did warn our friends and allies about the impending dangers of Putin. This has been in the making for the last 12 or more years. So as far as I am concerned, I keep telling people, just because I am a Hungarian, I might still be right about Vladimir Putin.

But I would like to echo what Edward said, that first of all he is not interested in the long, long, long, long-term success of Russia because what you are talking about is a very long, difficult, painful, bloody process, which at the end of the day will be the best for the Russian people. What he is interested in is the next 20 years. He wants to stay in power for the next 20 years, and we are the biggest threat to his continuous remaining in power, because transparency, accountability, and the rule of law means that he will end up where almost all authoritarian leaders or dictators end up, and that is something he wants to prevent.

Senator JOHNSON. So understanding his goal—and I totally agree with that. This is all about one man, one man's power for the rest of his life. What is the best way to blunt that? What is the best way to confront that? What is the first thing we should do, the most effective thing, the thing that we can do and implement quickly?

Mr. SIMONYI. Let me just say that it is counterintuitive: The harder we react, the stronger our reaction. The more determined we are, the more likely he is to back off.

Senator JOHNSON. By the way, when we were in Poland, and again I do not want to name the official, this individual said that the main reason Vladimir Putin did not go further into Eastern Ukraine is because he was genuinely surprised at the West's reaction. We had bipartisan senatorial delegations. The West actually covered what he was doing. Basically, this Polish official credited the West's reaction that surprised Putin for having him hold off. So that basically bolsters your point.

Mr. SIMONYI. Yes, but it could have been a little harder.

Senator JOHNSON. Absolutely.

Mr. SIMONYI. And Senator, that would have given us a lot more time to fix the problem.

Senator JOHNSON. I think our reaction has been totally weak, totally lacked resolve, totally inadequate.

Go ahead, Mr. Chow.

Mr. CHOW. First of all, I want to agree with my fellow panelists that Mr. Putin clearly has different metrics for success than we hold. But I also want to say that he is not insensitive to the down sides of what his action has caused. I see the deal that he signed with the Chinese in Shanghai on May 21, for example, as a reaction. It is not going to help him in the short run, but it is a reaction to the need to show that Russia cannot be isolated and his need for a political win in the foreign policy and trade sphere.

So the fact that he may think that he is winning does not mean that we should give up. I think the steadfastness of Western policy is the most important thing. Here I would repeat again what I said in my oral testimony earlier, that strengthening Ukraine, helping Ukraine become a democratic and prosperous free market country, is the best thing that we could be doing in the short to medium term.

Senator JOHNSON. I totally agree. By the way, I think what we should be doing is everything we can to bolster energy and Poroshenko's hand—help provide advisers, provide military equipment if so requested. I mean real military equipment, things that actually might change the balance, change the calculus.

Ms. Shaffer.

Dr. SHAFFER. I think we should not equate Russia's recent actions just with Putin's personality and his specific goals. I think actually any Russian leadership would try to invade Crimea. After the invasion of Crimea there was an interesting debate in the United States: Is this the return of geopolitics? In my years as an international relations specialist, the idea of the return of geopolitics is like saying, oh, the return of the Pacific Ocean, or the return of the Caucasus Mountains. Of course geopolitics is always there, and the only thing that changes, we try, as Mr. Lucas pointed out, we try to ignore them.

E.H. Carr, who I think was the most important strategist of the 20th century, said that the most dangerous way of analyzing politics is the world as you would like it to be, versus as it is. The Soviet breakup left Crimea, left the Black Sea fleet, outside the jurisdiction of Russia. I am not saying on an ethical level this was nice, to invade another country. But this was almost like leaving the Pacific fleet outside, if California broke off from the United States and leaving the Pacific fleet outside the jurisdiction of the United States. It was a ticking bomb.

The only problem, as some of our panelists have pointed out, we did not learn any lessons about how countries react. Actually, there is something connecting these panels in terms of natural gas, because states are like natural gas. They expand as much as they can until they hit some kind of container.

Basically, Russia saw this as the opportunity, this was the timing. But invading Crimea was something that was always going to happen. We have seen it. This is the Russian playbook. I think that why they seem to be pulling back from Ukraine is that it gets us focusing on eastern Ukraine, forgetting about Crimea. This is the same thing they did when they invaded Georgia. It seems like they are going to invade Tbilisi when they have no intent to invade it. Then you are very happy when they stay just in Abkhazia and South Ossetia. It seems like they are going to invade Azerbaijan and then you are very happy when they just want to stay in the region as peacekeepers.

So I think this is their playbook, is to get us focusing on getting them out of eastern Ukraine so we will not really remember that they actually are staying in Crimea.

Senator JOHNSON. Vladimir Putin is playing the West like a violin because we refuse to acknowledge reality. We continue to deny reality, trying to rely on hope as being a strategy, and hope is not. We have to be very brutal in our assessment of what the reality of the situation is. That is why I keep going back to having to recognize that Vladimir Putin's goal really is his power, his control. That is right, I do personalize it more, because it makes no sense for his country, for the citizens of Russia. It makes total sense when he wants to maintain his own personal power for as long as he lives.

Dr. SHAFFER. To respond to Senator Murphy's question about who is winning: Every day thousands of people are trying to enter the United States and they hope not only to enter here, but to stay here as legal citizens. I do not see thousands of people trying to break through the border and make it into Russia. So I think at the end of the day we can feel very comfortable. I agree we have to stop this defeatism in our policies.

Senator MURPHY. I thank the witnesses. Thank you, Ms. Shaffer, for that comment as well. Senator Johnson and I agree on much more than people may think when it comes to a lot of these topics. We obviously do disagree on right now the scorecard between the East and the West.

I will just close with this comment. There is some irony to Putin's actions. We both agree that there is short-term calculus being made here. Of course, Russia made its name over the last 200 years by being better than anybody else at playing the long game. It was Kutuzov who emptied out Moscow down to 10,000 residents in order to allow Napoleon to stretch his troops so far into the Russian territory that eventually his forces collapsed.

I think it is important for us to remember that the long game is creating a real contrast between what it means to align yourself with the West with free market economics and liberal democracy and what it ultimately means to be beholden to Russia. This is asymmetrical warfare right now. They are willing to use tactics that we simply are not willing to use. That may mean that we lose a couple skirmishes and battles along the way. But in the end the advertisement, by being the ones that are unwilling to engage in that kind of intimidation, bribery, and corruption, ultimately probably means that we now are the ones that hopefully will be able to win the long game.

Thank you very much for being here. With that, our hearing is adjourned. The record will remain open until Friday at 5 o'clock. We have other questions from committee members. We hope that you will turn around answers as quickly as possible.

[Whereupon, at 4:36 p.m., the hearing was adjourned.]

www.ingramcontent.com/pod-product-compliance
Lightning Source LLC
Chambersburg PA
CBHW052012280526

45793CB00005B/945

* 9 7 8 1 5 0 5 2 3 4 3 4 3 *